DIRTY GIRLS

DIRTY GIRLS

THE NAKED TRUTH ABOUT OUR GUILTY SECRETS*
*(UNPRETTY, UNCLEAN, AND UTTERLY HORRIFYING)

GILLIAN TELLING

sourcebooks
casablanca

Published by Sourcebooks Casablanca, an imprint of Sourcebooks, Inc.
P.O. Box 4410, Naperville, Illinois 60567-4410
(630) 961-3900
Fax: (630) 961-2168
www.sourcebooks.com

Library of Congress Cataloging-in-Publication Data

Telling, Gillian.
    Dirty girls : the naked truth about our guilty secrets (unpretty,
unclean, and utterly horrifying) / by Gillian Telling.
        p. cm.
    1. Women—Humor. 2. Sex—Humor. I. Title.
PN6231.W6T44 2010
814'.6—dc22
                                    2010010678

Printed and bound in the United States of America.
VP 10 9 8 7 6 5 4 3 2 1

For my twisted sisters, Claire, Mary, and Stephanie

Contents

Acknowledgments ix

Author's Note xi

Introduction xiii

Chapter One

The Single Woman May Be the Grossest
    Creature on the Planet 1

Chapter Two

Everyone Poops—Even Gisele Bündchen. 15

Chapter Three

A Perfectly Adequate Dinner: *Peanut Butter*
    on a Spoon. 27

Chapter Four

The Truth about Dirty Girls and Their Friends:
    I've Seen a Picture of My Best Friend's
    Boyfriend's Wiener 43

Chapter Five

Lies We Tell Men: *You Were the Best I Ever Had, and I've Only Slept with Nine People*. . . . 61

Chapter Six

DJ Diddle: *The Reality of Women, Masturbation, and Porn*. 89

Chapter Seven

Picking Up Dirty Girls: *We Are Far More Complicated Than Men Think*. 111

Chapter Eight

What Women Want in Bed: *Put Down the* Kama Sutra *Because There's No Way We're Doing the Wheelbarrow with You Tonight* 137

Chapter Nine

When Dirty Girls Fall In Love—And When They Fall Out of It 169

Chapter Ten

The End Game: *How Dirty Girls Really Feel about Happily Ever After* 191

About the Author 217

Acknowledgments

I'd like to thank all my filthy girlfriends who happily contributed their shameless stories to this book. Though I do not want to out them, in no particular order I'd like to acknowledge Erin, Amelia, Corinne, Susie, Lauren, Teri, Lesley, Lindsey, and Erica for being hilarious, disgusting, and inspiring women. I'd also like to thank Maria Fontoura, Jim Kaminsky, and Joe Levy for being my awesome editors at *Maxim*, and Shana Drehs for being my awesome editor at Sourcebooks. Thanks also to Daniel Greenberg, agent extraordinaire, and to Josh for not asking to read this before it was published. Please don't leave me.

Author's Note

Warning: This book has been written by a self-described Dirty Girl and is to be read by other Dirty Girls—girls who will revel in seeing their hidden secrets uncovered in print. This book was *not* intended to be read by men, unless they want to shatter all illusions of what they think women are like. Ladies, if you would prefer to have your man continue thinking you are pretty and perfect in every way, please keep this book away from him at all costs. Or if you would like to clue him in on a few things related to your private behavior, you can casually leave the book laying around, with the pages dog-eared or with Post-it Notes tagging certain sections. Just remember this: if you do let him read this, he will probably not look at you in the same way ever again. This could be a good or a bad thing, depending on how much you actually like getting laid. You have been warned. You may proceed.

Introduction

So, ladies…

As you know, men are from Mars and women are from Venus. Actually, some old fart coined that catchy title years ago to sell millions of books, and, well, he totally succeeded in selling millions of books. And desktop calendars. And even those miniature books that no one really wants but gets in their stockings at Christmas every year. Good for him. But what he also did was spawn an entire generation of men and women who treat this catchy title as though it were the word of God. Because it explains everything! No wonder men and women have so many issues trying to get along well with one another! How on earth are we supposed to be friends and lovers when we obviously come from completely different planets? Guys aren't even the same *species* as us. They're Martians! Basically, asking men and women to get along as human beings is like asking a native San Franciscan to stop talking about how delicious the burritos are there. It's simply not natural.

But is it really that simple? Men and women can have vast differences in their outlooks and actions. That's not a total shocker. But what I have found in the past few years of writing a sex column for *Maxim* magazine, for which I have interviewed countless women about their lives, dirty secrets, and dreams for the future, is that women are actually not all that different from men. They seem to want the same things out of life as the opposite sex does: success, health, friendship, money, a career, a functional family, functioning relationships, a good body, and lots and lots of great sex. Women want to have fun and are funny, and they can be nasty, horny, brutish little buggers at the same time.

Don't get me wrong—I'm not trying to say women are the new men. We don't *want* to be men. Why would we want to be men? Lower salaries and suffering through nine months of sobriety during pregnancy notwithstanding, for the most part, it's pretty good being us. I'm just saying we're just so much more similar to guys than anyone has ever admitted. Until *now*. The jig is up, sisters. I'm exposing us, in this book, for the filthy, funny, picky, generous, cruel, nasty, beautiful beasts we really are.

Chapter One

The Single Woman May Be the Grossest Creature on the Planet

A very basic fact about women, one that we spend an awful lot of time hiding behind lip gloss and brushed hair and spritzes of sweet-smelling perfume, is that we are very often just straight up *nasty*. By that, I don't mean we are crazy and wild in the sack—I mean we are disgustingly gross. As in this: we've all had a pair of jeans we've washed maybe once or twice in all the months or years of wearing them, and we all do things like wear our bikini bottoms for underpants when we've neglected to do laundry and have run out of clean panties (or we turn our dirty panties inside out—or we don't wear any at all). But we've spent years hiding these kinds of facts from men, who seem to think we're all well put together and probably wear lacy matching bra-and-undie sets every day.

You can imagine what goes through a naive man's mind when he sees a sexy young thing at the end of the bar giving him the come-hither look. He probably thinks that she smells like vanilla Rice Krispie Treats, her lips taste like SweeTarts, and her perfectly decorated apartment will have lots of artfully arranged pillows on the bed and be drowning in vases of tulips. Maybe she'll even have homemade lemon bars on hand for a postcoital snack!

But the truth is, if she's really single, and she *really* takes him back to her place for some delicious lovemaking, he needs to prepare himself for when he walks through her doors. It might be the bare fridge that only has two bottles of Sauvignon Blanc and a stick of butter in it, the faint stench of cat litter that lingers even though there doesn't appear to be a cat, or a door that she warns him not to open. The reality is, this girl is not perfect. This girl is probably actually pretty *gross*, and in all honesty, in many ways she is probably much worse than the guy.

Or at least most of the women I know are.

Real Women and Hygiene

Here's a riddle for you: if a woman comes home at two in the morning, eats an entire box of mac and cheese, drops the dirty pans in the sink, strips to nothing but her socks, and goes to bed without brushing her teeth, and no one is around to see it, did it really happen? (Hint: nope.)

Here's the first real truth men don't know about women. When we're single, when we don't have to be responsible for anyone but ourselves, and when we are in the privacy of our own home, we are pretty filthy creatures. Were a man ever to catch a single woman in her natural habitat—say, lying in bed on a Sunday morning, lazily watching E! and eating some cold pizza off her chest—then he would see us women as we truly are: lazy and loving it.

The reason men aren't fully aware of the jungle beasts within us is because the woman who lives with her boyfriend or husband will do her best to keep the house looking presentable, and for the most part, she will do her best to make *herself* presentable: toothpaste, lipstick, hair brushing, occasionally shaving her legs, showering—sigh. She will get up before 9 a.m. on the weekend and make coffee, maybe even breakfast, and will read the paper and wander around her neighborhood with her beau, buying overpriced things from overpriced stores with him. She will say things like "dinner party" and "armoire." She will act as if she were put together, a proper adult with a proper schedule to keep, and a guy will find this impressive and enjoyable because it also keeps his disgusting inner self at bay.

However, the woman who doesn't live with her significant other will totally unleash her filthy beast when he's not around. For the men reading this, you may want to keep that in mind should you ever decide to drop by around 11 a.m. on a Sunday with a basket full of bagels. (Yes, we do realize you're actually *never* going to come around with a basket full of bagels on a Sunday morning, which is why we're not going to put in our contact lenses or even put our pants on. Also, if you did this, let's face it, we would probably think you were gay.) But let's just say if you *were* to drop by with a basket of bagels, you'd probably find us eating Fruity Pebbles by the fistful from the box, staring at bad TV, and absentmindedly scratching our crotches with our free hands. Sound familiar?

How the Single Woman Keeps Her House

The other day I asked one of my friends if she wanted me to come over and hang out at her place. She lives alone, and I like to bring big fat bottles of wine over, sit at her kitchen table, smoke cigarettes, and talk shit about work, families, love, and sometimes other people we know. Normally she readily agrees, but this time she hesitated.

"No, you can't come by," she said.

"Why, what are you doing?" I asked.

"Um, I'm cleaning…" she said, obviously lying.

"Gross! Are you masturbating?" I asked her.

"No, I'm just really busy and had to organize some boxes and…well, OK, fine, my house is too messy for guests, actually," she said. "It's disgusting. I haven't cleaned it in like two months. And I think I have moths."

"Are you sure they're not weevils?" I asked. "I had weevils in my dry goods once."

"No, they're definitely moths," she sighed. "Big, disgusting gray moths, and they're everywhere."

"Well, I don't mind the moths if you don't," I said. "I want to hang out."

"OK, sure. Come over. But you're not allowed to go into the back part of the apartment," she warned.

"No problem."

"And don't tell anyone that I have moths."

"Yeah, don't worry. I won't."

• • •

My friend is not the only single woman in the world who can let her house or apartment get to such an unusually nasty level of disarray that she suffers from a pest infestation. I know two lesbians (yes, two girls!) who have pubic hair balls in the corner of their bathroom that would impress a frat brother. Until they have a wine fridge and regularly entertain other pals with their beau, most women are generally too busy earning a paycheck day to day, being social, going to the gym (OK, *sometimes* going to the gym), and occasionally even taking in a movie or something cultural to keep a perfect fucking house. In a nutshell, we don't have any more time than busy dudes do to be homemakers anymore. And if no one is around to judge us about our inner filthy beasts, then why should we care?

We don't.

That's one thing men have never known about us. We have perfected the art of organized piles and stuffing dirty things in closets in case they are coming over. Plus, we all know about the miracles of Febreze and scented candles (whoever created those awesome products was definitely a Dirty Girl). But we all have a secret disgusting side, and we are certainly not all programmed to be good homemakers. This is something learned, and honestly, sometimes forced, once we find ourselves in a relationship. The real woman cannot just whip up a delicious brunch on a whim from items in her fridge and cupboards. She does not have eggs (maybe some old ones that she's scared to crack open), she does not have milk, and she does not have cheese (that isn't moldy in the corner at least), so she cannot make an omelet. There is no package of bacon, either in the fridge or frozen, awaiting the exciting day she might decide to make a big brunch. There *might* be bread, because peanut butter toast is always a good breakfast (or lunch or dinner). A man, if he's lucky enough to be brought home with this woman for the night, should just be prepared to splurge on brunch the next morning.

The Single Woman and Personal Hygiene

For single women, weekends are truly delightful because we get to shun our regular bathing routines. We love nothing more than shunning this routine. We pride ourselves on being soap dodgers on lazy weekends. And not having to deal with wet hair... what a blessing. If we can just scrape those strands up into a greasy bun or ponytail, we are happy humans. If we don't have to put on deodorant or shave our pits or pluck our eyebrows or Q-tip our ears or put on perfume or even put on makeup, all the better. Of course, this is if we are lounging around alone or with other women indoors. If we are going out in public, it's likely we'll gloss ourselves up a bit. We may be lazy and unhygienic at heart, but we are also vain creatures, and vanity trumps laziness. But if no one is around who cares what we look like, then we certainly don't care.

My mom actually used to ask me to shower when I'd go home to Florida for Christmas. "But I went to the beach and got in the ocean earlier!" I'd protest, even though I was twenty-five and old enough to know that regular bathing is considered the norm at that age. That's me, though. I decided that, to make sure I wasn't the only gal who relished rolling around in my own filth anytime I didn't have to be in public or look pretty for a boy, I would check in with my most pristine friends to ask what their weekend cleanliness habits were like.

Bianca, twenty-eight years old, is one of the most high-achieving women I know. She is smart, strong, funny, and very successful in her line of work. She's always dressed impeccably in the latest styles, and her hair is always perfectly flat ironed with silky bangs that swoosh off to the side. In short, she's one of those magazine girls who actually exist in real life. But because she's so funny and nice, her physical perfection is not annoying in the least. However, I've known Bianca for a long time and know that she sometimes abuses prescription drugs and once got strep throat after giving head to a friend of mine with a dirty dick. In short, she's not allowed to pretend to be perfect around me.

So, Bianca gave it to me straight up: "I usually don't shower on either Saturday or Sunday," she said. "The only time I do is if I have a date or have to go somewhere nice, but even then a lot of times I'm just doing the old deodorant and hairbrush routine. Showering is a pain in the ass, and I hate having wet hair."

Validation! I once managed four days without showering. Did you know that after the third day, your greasy hair corrects itself and actually looks *clean* again?

It's not simply showering that I've avoided for lengths at a time when I didn't feel like anyone around me actually gave a shit. I also avoided shaving. It wasn't that I purposefully avoided it or thought, "Mwahaha! I'm not going to shave because I can get away with being a furry beast!" It just didn't cross my mind. Or maybe there wasn't a razor around and I was too forgetful to buy a new one or too lazy to step out of the shower and dig around under the sink for a spare. This means that I have gone fairly long with new underarm growth and hairy legs and a bush straight out of a 1970s porn. Shaving is something we do because we want to get *laid*. Not because it makes us feel better about ourselves as women.

Speaking of getting laid, these days it's not enough to just shave your hairiness from time to time. Now we need to regularly partake in grooming. Ugh. For most women, this is a touchy subject. We can't help but feel a little put out by it. It's a pain in the ass to always look cute. Still, we want to be beautiful and have silky legs and shiny hair and tiny hair triangles in our nether-regions to impress potential sexual partners, but that takes a lot of work, not to mention a lot of money and a lot of unnecessary pain. I shall hereby explain the process of getting a Brazilian bikini wax, just so your man knows what you go through in getting them. And then maybe he'll take extra care in admiring your trim and tidy lady parts and your entirely well-kept body. Please dog-ear this passage and put it on your lover's pillow tonight.

HAVE YOUR MAN READ THIS, PLEASE: BRAZILIAN WAX, THE REAL STORY

Enter salon. Tell the woman you're here for your Brazilian. Go into a tiny room with a doctor's bed in it that's topped with that crinkly hygiene paper. Drop trou and underpants, keeping socks and shirts on (awkward, but better than being totally naked). Smile at woman as she comes in and sits with her face a mere two inches from your private parts and begins probing you with gloved fingers to assess the hairy mess. Worry whether you smell or are horrifying her with your monthlong pubic hair growth. Feel shame. Start to feel nervous because suddenly hot (and I mean *hot*) wax is being spread mere millimeters from your labia. Feel sick as you realize cloth is being pressed onto the wax and the pain is about to come. Feel sheer burning agony from your toes to your eyeballs as she yanks out five hundred coarse and curly hairs in one fell swoop. See stars. Clutch crotch. Want to puke. Groan. Beg her to stop. Listen to her cackle at you while she says it's not *that* bad and you have lots of hairs to go. Repeat this process for ten more yanks. After each brutal rip, when you're sure skin has come off each time, face the humiliation of having the waxer *show* you just how much hair she got each time. ("Look at it, see? Lots of hairs!") Feel utter relief when it is finally done. Then total horror hits all over again as you realize she's now *plucking* rogue hairs out of your anus—with tweezers. Try not to cry. Think about how sex will feel so good and how much your man will love it. Look down at her handiwork, and...Oh my God, is that *blood*? Suddenly hate your man and the paternal society we live in that dictates we have to look like prepubescent porn stars. Curse him and *his* massive pubic fro. Bastard. Vow to dump him. Pay $60. Limp home. Try to pull underwear off of sticky vagina. Face ingrown hairs over the next couple of weeks and the unsightly, hair-pluggy look of regrowth and silently weep as you realize it's time for another visit to the Meanie Pants Pube Waxer.

• • •

So, now you men know. This is not fun for us. It is not cheap for us. And yes, we agree that sex is better after we have it done, but mainly because you are that much more willing to go down on us for lengthy periods of time, and we really like that. But if we didn't have to do it, we wouldn't. Sure, nobody has to do it. But it's become the norm, and when we don't have some sort of grooming action happening down there, we feel like Sasquatch and are embarrassed by how poofy au naturel looks. Still, if you want her to keep it up, you'd better heap on the praise each time your woman comes home from this. And you'd better get on your knees and pray to that hairless altar—until we tell you you're allowed to come up for air.

Chapter Two

Everyone Poops—
Even Gisele Bündchen

Remember that book we all read when we were kids called *Everyone Poops*? It featured a little boy who was learning how to use a toilet and talked about how rabbits pooped, cats pooped, and even giraffes pooped! Yeah—giraffes. But what was the one thing it didn't mention? *Girls* who pooped. I mean, come on! Even beautiful flawless women like Gisele Bündchen will have to take a mean dump after some scoops of Monday Night Football chili at the Brady household. But men don't— won't—believe this to be true. And women sadly spend a ridiculous amount of time trying to hide this basic fact of nature from men. I am terribly guilty of this myself.

During the first year of one of my relationships, I managed to not drop *le deuce* at my new boyfriend's apartment, not even once. To do this, I endured crippling cramps in the mornings as I rushed to work, where I could use the office toilet in peace. Occasionally, if things were a little, um, rough, I would tell him I was dying for a soda and would run to the third floor of his apartment building, where there was a gym, a soda machine, and a toilet. I can't tell if he would have been less disturbed by the fact that I was human and needed to crap than by the fact that he thought I liked Coca-Cola at 7:30 in the morning. But I had a secret to keep, and I would go to great lengths to make sure he did not know I was human and took the occasional dump. Sadly, my secret didn't last for long. I'd confessed to a few friends my dilemma of wanting to remain pretty and perfect for his benefit and my cursed morning gas cramps. "It's a real problem, I tell you," I said to them.

"Oh, please, how could you not just crap at his place? Everybody poops!" they all cried out. Yes, I know. But you see, I don't just poop. I chill out. I hang out for twenty minutes, reading the backs of shampoo bottles and old Archie comics.

Sometimes—and this is pretty foul—I even text people or play a game on my cell phone if I have some time to kill. I'm not from the school of the old in-and-out. I never have been, and I can't start now—hence my unwillingness to do my leisurely biz at his place. Also, pretty and polished women aren't supposed to do disgusting things like that!

Lucky for me, one of my closest (and, it turns out, cruelest) friends decided it was time for this pretty-and-perfect charade to come to an end. So one day when we were all at a house we'd rented in Vermont for the week of New Year's, I whispered to my buddy that I was going to sneak off to the basement loo for some bathroom alone time, with *Cosmo* magazine hidden under my shirt like a boy off to spank it to a catalog. I'd just gotten settled in for a nice quiet half hour and was reading a tip on how to outline your lips to make them look poutier when the door suddenly flew open. There stood my boyfriend alongside my bitchy (might as well tell you now that he is gay) friend.

"I just wanted you to know that Gillian shits," said my friend to my boyfriend. I'm not sure who was more distraught. The boyfriend, for seeing me chilling out and reading *Cosmo* while taking a dump, or me, for suddenly realizing that I had the worst taste in friends in the world.

"Get out!" I screamed while lunging for the door. They slammed it, and I could hear them go back up the stairs. I sat there for a few minutes with my head in my hands, willing evil, cruel death on my friend and praying that my boyfriend just thought I was peeing. Still, I eventually had to get up and face him. I caught up with him in the kitchen.

"I'm really sorry. That was, um, weird," I said, mortified. He was a little red-faced too, but very sweet about it.

"Well, it's not a total shock that you crap," he said. "I figured you did at least occasionally. Don't worry about it." So it all turned out OK. But I still spent the next few months doing my biz at his gym, and I did not forgive my friend for a very long time. I was cruelly gleeful when he told me that a man he had picked up in Berlin told him he had a small penis.

Girl Talk

It's not news that women have the same bodily functions as men, but what guys definitely don't know is how often and freely we talk about this among ourselves when they're not in the room. Why, you might ask, do we talk about this so much? For the same reason that men and children do. It's funny. The other day, as I sat down to my office computer around 10 a.m., a Google Chat window popped up. It was about ten in the morning, and this is what my friend wanted to tell me: "Yo. I just took a two-foot shit."

I paused, thinking about how to respond to this message so early in the morning. Naturally, there was only one way: "Awesome! Seriously two feet?"

"Yeah, I'm literally five pounds lighter."

"Ah, I love those."

"But seriously, Gillian, it was two feet long with no breakage whatsoever. It just floated there. It was incredible."

"Man, I kinda wish I'd seen it."

"I know. I wish I'd taken a picture."

"Next time, please do."

This, you see, is not exactly an unusual conversation for me and the women in my life. A few months ago, a group of girlfriends and I were having drinks and listening to one of our friends talk about how she had had such a terrible bout of the runs that she had actually gotten some on the *walls*.

"Ew!" we all cried, laughing.

"Yeah," she said. "It was horrible. It looked like a Jackson Pollock painting."

"You mean a Jackson Poolock?" said another.

"Maybe it was more like a Poocasso," suggested another.

"It was probably form the doo-doo era," I chimed in. As we sat around this public bar laughing about her diarrhea, I realized that men don't know how much women talk this way. As a rule, women *never* discuss with men the shape, color, or stench of anything that they might consider gross. Get us alone, though, and we're a bunch of foul beasts. When nature calls, one friend says she's "gotta take a trip to the dump can," and another says she's "gonna motor to the shitter." These expressions are not what men would expect chicks to say, especially ones who are both beautiful and successful and the perfect picture of classy ladies. However, the moment these women are sans men, they are grosser than a bunch of farty frat dudes.

In fact, I had a friend over recently, who actually asked me to pull her finger. I did it and then totally laughed as she beefed. This same friend called me a few years ago to tell me that she had sharted—when you fart and a little fudge comes out—in a cab on her way home.

"Who cares, you don't know the cabbie," I assured her.

"No, you don't understand. My boss was in the cab with me. And I *told* her I sharted because I figured she could smell it. I am now going to get fired because I crapped my pants and then told my boss what happened!" For the record, she didn't get fired. Well, not immediately.

In case you suspect I am particularly immature when it comes to disgusting bodily matters, think about this: after I wrote a *Maxim* column on women who like to have sex outdoors and in other public spaces, I found that a lot of women also liked to do other biz with Mother Nature as well.

"I also prefer to piss outside," said a woman I spoke to, when she told me she loved having sex in her backyard and in public parks. "So maybe I just like doing everything better outdoors." This wasn't the first I'd heard of this. One night, at a summer backyard barbecue, I was chatting away with a new friend when she announced she had to pee. I expected her to go to the house, but instead she walked a few feet into the garden and copped a squat. She continued talking to me as she watered the lawn.

"Sorry," she said. "I know the bathroom is close, but I actually prefer going outside if it's more convenient."

I understood completely. When I was a kid, I actually preferred crapping outside and had my favorite bush for such purposes. However, I stopped once my mom caught me and threatened to rub my nose in it. But, really, why waste ten minutes doing something that really takes only two? Modern plumbing is a miracle not to be scoffed at, but if a guy was hanging out outside with only other men, there's no way he'd wander around looking for an indoor toilet if he had to wee. From what I've discovered, a good percentage of women feel the same way.

Most women told me that peeing outside was a matter of convenience. And Dirty Girls are usually down for anything that saves time and energy. At clubs in college, my friends and I would always duck outside to a parking lot to pee instead of waiting in the long lines inside. We'd sit on the bumpers of cars or on the curb. Then we'd go right back into the clubs, no harm no foul. OK, well maybe a little foul.

The High Cost of Gas

One thing women will always try to control in front of men is their farts. However, this is uncomfortable, and we relieve ourselves of such bloated pressure any chance we get. When there is no guy in our beds, we freely let farts rip. But when we spend each night with a boyfriend or husband, we often have to make special trips to the toilet to toot, or we try to do it quickly when they are out of the room—like when your guy is in the shower or brushing his teeth and you squeak one out and then violently flap the sheets to clear the air before he returns. This happens in bedrooms all across America, night after night.

A good way for the casual observer to tell whether a woman is sneakily cutting the cheese when she's walking around with a guy is if she suddenly pauses to look at some obscure sign or poster in a window. If she is intensely reading a flyer for free viola lessons, chances are she's just lingering by that telephone pole to pass gas. She'll catch up when she's ready—heaven forbid he should turn and go back to her, lest he gets there before the fart has wafted and busts her in an uncomfortable and stinky moment.

If we do accidentally fart in front of a guy, we pray he'll either do the polite thing and ignore it or be funny and gracious and handle it with a laugh and a tease. "Did someone step on a duck?" is sure to get us giggling. Making a gross-out face and saying "Ew!" is not a cool way to deal with this situation. I once spent two years in a relationship with a guy without ever once breaking wind in front of him. And then I did. We were on the street, and I was convinced that the traffic noise would cover the sound, but he heard it, dropped my hand, and said, "Gross!" Don't get me wrong, I loved him, but the fact that he was horrified that I accidentally beefed triggered some questions for me. Did he have absurd expectations about what women were allowed and not allowed to do to remain sexy and feminine? Needless to say, we broke up a short while later. I certainly won't blame the downfall of our relationship on my gassy slip-up, but his reaction definitely made him a lot less cool, especially because I'd never said anything about the times his violently hot and spicy farts woke me up in the middle of the night after we'd eaten Thai food.

HAVE YOUR MAN READ THIS, PLEASE: AUNT FUCKING FLO'S IN TOWN

There is one *very* special thing that happens to women that does not happen to men. And men do not like to hear about it, talk about it, or even remotely think about it.

That's right. I'm talking about our periods.

Periods suck for us. They happen month after month, year after year, for up to fifty years! They are painful and troublesome, they ruin our clothes, and we have to spend lots of money on products to control them. But at the same time, they remind us that we are capable of creating human beings in our bellies, which is both incredibly weird and awesome. Still, periods freak out men. I get why—it's blood, and nothing is freakier than blood. Blood means pain, cuts, and dying. But bear in mind that a period is nothing more than a woman shedding a microscopic egg from her body, and there is no wound or pain in sight. Well, except for those damn cramps—in which case you should be nice and get us Advil.

If you want to understand what a woman

means when she says, "I have cramps," then imagine this: You go to the ballpark hungover, eat two dogs, and wash them down with a bunch of light beer. Yeah. Shit cramps. The kind that make you double over and sweat with the hair on your arms standing on end until you reach a toilet. Take cramps seriously.

Some women don't like sex when they have their period, but others don't mind it and some love it. If you're not squeamish and neither is she, I applaud you. Lay down towels before you start rocking each other's worlds. But never make a woman feel bad or gross because it's that time of the month. We can't help it, and it's how you were born, loser.

Chapter Three

A Perfectly Adequate Dinner

Peanut Butter on a Spoon

Women have always had an interesting relationship with food. Basically, we love it. We love to eat it, we love to go out to fancy dinners and eat fancy meals, we love it when we have someone fun to cook for who thinks everything we make is delicious, and we especially love it when someone cooks for us and the end result actually *is* delicious and we don't have to pretend. (I once chomped through the foulest lasagna I have ever tasted on a date where the guy cooked and claimed, "So delicious!" when I actually wanted to puke.) But for most women, sometimes nothing in the world makes us happier than squishing on the couch with a giant bowl of our favorite comfort food (for me this is either mac and cheese or Lucky Charms) and curling up for a giant, no-holds-barred chomping-down session. And when I say nothing is better, I mean *nothing*. No man, no sex, no raise in your paycheck will seem better than whatever is in your bowl in front of you.

Unfortunately, because women are complicated freaks, we also tend to have bad relationships with food. (What? No relationship is perfect.) We hate what our favorite snacks do to our asses and thighs, we hate that salads and everything good for you never fills us up the way pizza does, we hate that carbs are undoubtedly the most delicious things in the universe, and we hate that food can really show what bad homemakers we are or how terrible we are at taking care of ourselves. We are supposed to keep fresh fruits and veggies and string cheese and yogurt on hand at all time for snacks. Maybe a handful of raw almonds when we're feeling peckish! But I don't know a single woman who actually adheres to this way of living, for more than a week or two, anyway. Especially the Dirty Girls I know. Almonds? Sure, but we get those salted wasabi tins of them and down them in a single sitting.

How We Feel about Cooking

Foodies, locavores, *Julie & Julia*—these are all phenomena that couples get excited about. Couples *love* to peruse the farmers market hand in hand, excitedly waiting for heirloom tomato and sweet corn season to dawn so they can make fresh and tasty things like salsas and compotes and then eat them together and feel proud of their delicious accomplishments. I know one couple whose world simply revolves around what they are making for breakfast, lunch, and dinner, and they post these meals as their Facebook status updates. Sometimes with photos. And they are always really weird and complicated meals, like bone marrow simmered in the broth of a baby goat's uterus. They also like to brag that their baby is already a "foodie" who just loves foie gras and raw hamachi.

Single women, however, have a weird thing about cooking. We of course love a good home-cooked meal, but we hate buying, preparing, and cleaning it up afterward if we're the only ones eating. We try to go to the farmers market too, but it's kind of depressing seeing all those couples buying basil plants together. Plus, when we buy heirloom tomatoes, they'll most likely rot because we are going out to dinner again instead of making heirloom tomato salad. Cooking for one is just such a pain in the ass. Ordering in, going out, or thawing some Amy's enchiladas is easier and frankly more fun and tastier. If we don't have some friends or a guy we like oohing and ahhing over our grandma's delicious roast chicken recipe, why on earth would we bother to cook it? We won't. On rare occasions, I really do cook something just for myself. Although I try to make it healthy and well balanced, it usually ends up being some version of pasta with lots of butter, Parmesan, and salt. And in that case, I might as well just have mac and cheese, right?

Having a nutritious lunch can be easier because going out to lunch every day isn't frowned on, and it's easier to get veggies in at midday. But this is if you work at an office near a lot of lunch places. I once worked from home for a few months, and without a designated lunch break to pick something up from a nearby deli, I had a hard time making myself eat well during the day—strictly because I was lazy. I never had bread, mayo, or deli meats on hand to make a tasty little sandwich. I had some beer and limes and three half-full, rotten tubs of Penang curry that I'd ordered from a local Thai joint over the past three weeks. But other than that, I had nothing for lunch. I didn't even have ingredients to make eggs (say, eggs) or pizza muffins, my favorite college staple.

So for me, lunch always meant either going hungry or going out somewhere. That somewhere was the nearby bar with free wi-fi. I could work from there and then get a beer, because how awkward would it be if I were in a bar and didn't order a beer? This usually turned into two beers and hurrying home to lean out the window and smoke some cigs from my emergency pack. Then I'd go out for more drinks during happy hour and come home late at night with two slices of pizza. It wasn't the most nutritious time in my life, but most women have been there. Cooking for one just sucks.

Drinking and Eating

When I worked at *Rolling Stone*, the women I worked with all became acutely aware of when someone was hungover, just from our various breakfast choices. One girl would guzzle a Coca-Cola. I'd stuff a bagel with American cheese, nuke it, and dip it in mustard. Another would roll in with McDonald's. We did not bring in Tupperware containers with homemade tuna sandwiches. We were single girls who went out at night instead of pureeing soups, and then would support one another during the day with meatball subs or street meat from a nearby cart. But this did not bode well with our typical food goal: trying as hard as we could to eat healthy meals so we wouldn't become lard asses.

The problem with drinking a lot is that you really don't think about food or your food choices, and you don't generally make healthy decisions, because sometimes you need penne à la vodka for breakfast in the worst way after a night of boozing and nothing else will suffice. I have a friend who usually doesn't eat dinner if she's out drinking after work, except for maybe snacking on the shared plate of nachos at the bar or a handful of bar nuts. This means she is doubly hungry the next morning—and needs to carboload ASAP to help curb the hangover and stabilize. So she always orders Italian for breakfast—or occasionally a pizza pie. Healthy? No. Normal? Totally. My favorite thing to eat when I've had too much to drink, other than the aforementioned bagel, is Thai curry and spring rolls. Lucky for me, I've learned to live with the odd looks the delivery guys would give me at 11 a.m. And lucky for me, they didn't stop delivering just because I once called them crying because they forgot to bring me my Coke.

"I'm the queen of binge eating after a big night out and then feeling so guilty about how unhealthy I've been that I force myself to eat something gross like lentils to make up for it the next day," says Emi. "There is no worse punishment for treating your body poorly than having to eat a microbiotic lunch."

The Food Guilts

One reason our issues with grub suck so much is that they just make us feel so damn *guilty* all the time. It's just another thing that we figure we are doing wrong (on top of not going to the gym regularly or still having to occasionally ask our parents for a rent loan). We all *try* to buy salad stuff, bags of baby carrots, and yogurt drinks, and then convince ourselves week after week that *this* week we'll pack tasty salads and low-fat turkey sandwiches for lunch. We lay in bed at night, night after night, and tell ourselves that we'll wake up early, do that yoga DVD, and make a nutritious smoothie. But it just never seems to happen, and day after day, we end up with a coffee and croissant from the bakery and spend $12 on takeout sushi for lunch—and then go out for happy hour with some friends where we all split one or two plates of mozzarella sticks, again. If it tastes so good, is that really so wrong?

Fear of Fat and Exercise

As a woman in her early thirties who surrounds herself with other like-minded, professional women (i.e., they have regular jobs but don't necessarily act like professionals all the time), I seem to know a lot of chicks who still have a crippling fear of fat and retain some obsessions with food that cannot always be categorized as "healthy." One friend regularly eats Adderalls because they keep not only her mood but also her weight in check. Another friend occasionally starves herself for the day in an effort to remain thin and chic. And who doesn't know someone who has been on a "cleanse," which is basically packaged and pricey starvation? These women *know* that what they're doing is not healthy. Everyone knows that the ideal way to maintain your fabulous body is to eat right and exercise regularly. But if that were so fucking easy to do, then would we have any kind of obesity problem in this country?

"I can't actually afford a gym," says my friend Marie, a magazine assistant editor. "My rent eats up half my paycheck, so the rest of it goes to bills and living life. I try to exercise outside here and there when it's warm enough, and I buy yoga DVDS, though they usually end up sitting on my bookshelf unopened. Truth is, I don't even know if I'd be good at going to the gym if I paid for one. I'd probably go for about a month and then get bored of it."

Most women I talked to echoed Marie's sentiment. If they already belonged to a gym, they did go, but never as much as they *should* go. They admitted that with a sense of foreboding. I can't tell you how many IM conversations I have with my girlfriends that go like this:

"UGH."

"What's up?"

"I have to go to the gym tonight but I reallllly don't want to go to the gym tonight. What are you doing?"

"Not going to the gym. Don't go if you're not in the mood."

"But I ate a huuuge lunch and I haven't been in three days and I'm going to have a super fat ass if I don't start going more."

"Ugh, I guess then just quickly go and get it over with?"

"But I reallllllyyy don't want to go. Do you want to grab a drink maybe?"

"Sure."

. . .

I ran into a problem myself when I joined an awesome, expensive gym in Rockefeller Center for a few months. The problem? The gym had a bar in it. No, not a juice bar—I'm talking a hidden gem of a real bar with nightly drink specials (like *good* glasses of wine for $5) and baskets of free popcorn to munch on. It overlooked the famous ice-skating rink, and on Thursdays there was even a DJ. The bar was never crowded, and it had plenty of comfortable seats. I started off just going to classes at the gym and enjoying my new healthy routine. Then I slowly started taking a day off from working out here and there and going to the bar to catch up with a friend or a co-worker. (The gym gave me drink passes when I started—it's the gym's fault, really). Soon I was forgoing classes altogether and hitting up the bar for wine and popcorn, looking guiltily away each time I saw the overachieving Swede from Zumba come and buy water after her workout. It was around that time that I realized the gym was far too expensive for me anyway and quit. I still pop by for drinks from time to time, though.

Cooking for the Newly Enlightened Guy

Like men, most women have at least one dish they can pull off reasonably well. But it's a total myth that women are decent cooks, even with the current foodie trend sweeping the nation that means everyone is excited about pickling root vegetables and growing herbs in an organic garden. In fact, most women I know say they find the foodie trend kind of annoying, mainly because guys have become so into cooking and meat and pickling things these days that they look unfavorably upon women who don't own their own set of German Wüsthof knives or have a Le Creuset Dutch oven.

"I was seeing a new guy, one of those New York renaissance dudes who is really into everything cultural, and of course is a big old foodie," says a friend of mine who eats out, orders in, or nukes a burrito almost every single night of the week. "I decided to cook for him, my one great dish, which is nothing more than store-made gnocchi in a creamy tomato sauce, but it always tastes amazing. Anyway, he came by and was watching as I was putting some Italian seasoning in the sauce, and he said, 'You should use fresh basil in that. I always add it in at the last minute when I make tomato sauces.' What the fuck? He was criticizing my cooking technique instead of being psyched I was making him a nice meal!"

I saw it live. She once invited me to a barbecue he was having, and he opened the meal (ribs) with an *amuse bouche*. Yes, a wee snack before the main meal. It wasn't substantial enough to be an appetizer, but the fact that he presented it as an *amuse bouche* was funny to me. My friend and I tried not to snicker. He then served up the ribs and placed bowls of warm liquid in front of us.

"What's this?" I asked, peering into the bowl in the darkness of the roof deck.

"It's not soup," he said.

"Nut soup?" I asked. "Wow, that sounds interesting."

"No, it's *not* soup," he said. "It's a finger bowl.

For your fingers." I watched him dab his fingers in the water, feeling like the unsophisticated hooker in *Pretty Woman* trying to eat snails. I caught the eye of my friend again, and we couldn't help but giggle. *Amuse bouche* and finger bowls? This was definitely the barbecue of a New York food snob. To test a theory, I mentioned that I was chilly and asked if he had a wrap I could borrow. I thought he might have a sweatshirt or jacket. He brought me a soft orange pashmina that was so cute I wanted to steal it.

Cleaning after Cooking Sucks More Than Cooking

I know a lot of women who, when they are in domestic relationships, take on the role of cooking just because it's infinitely more enjoyable to make the mess than it is to clean up the mess. And when you are the cook, you should be excused from the cleaning duties—if you are in charge of both cooking and cleaning, you need to have a talk with your mate. In some cases, when a guy hates to cook, this divide works out wonderfully. But not in one relationship of mine. My boyfriend was obviously the better cook, and I was screwed! He knew I couldn't resist his delicious Moroccan lamb stews, and so he would offer to whip up dinner. I'd be stuck scrubbing the pots and pans again. We didn't have a dishwasher, which made cleaning up all the more reprehensible. Washing dishes by hand is simply never, ever fun. This is why Dirty Girls often pile dishes in the sinks, especially when they live alone. Most of us don't scrub our coffee mug as soon as we use it. In fact, I suspect a lot of us leave half-empty coffee mugs around the kitchen, taking care of them only when little green fuzzies begin to float on the surface.

The Dirty Fridge

As proof of how disgusting humans are, a recent study has shown that the average person cleans the refrigerator only twice a year. I can tell you that the average woman who lives alone probably cleans hers out a lot less than that. Sure, she may toss all the moldy tubs of leftovers once in a while (and all those bags of spinach that never ended up in healthy salads to take to work), but she rarely gets on her hands and knees and scrubs out the inside of the fridge—or the oven, for that matter. In fact, the only time I recall cleaning the oven is when I accidentally melted a mouse glue trap in there. I'd forgotten it was there when I preheated the oven.

HAVE YOUR MAN READ THIS, PLEASE: THE TRUTH ABOUT WOMEN AND FOOD

When you are not around, we often eat gross things for dinner. The other night I had a plate of french fries and two glasses of wine. A few days before that, I had a bowl of cereal. This is not abnormal, and it's probably what you do too when no one is around to judge you.

"Sometimes I'll just have some peanut butter on a spoon," said one of my friends. Another admitted that her cupboards were so bare that for dinner she popped open an old bottle of champagne and had a few glasses of that with some stale marshmallows and cigarettes.

"I actually learned to like my coffee black because I had such a hard time keeping fresh milk or cream in my fridge," said another girl. "I guess it's good, it saves me a few calories!" But if you know a woman like this, don't ever make cracks about her bare cupboards or lack of fresh fruit.

When women are in relationships, we generally get over being so foul and might even start to enjoy cooking for you. If a woman does cook for you, though, and it's gross, do yourself a favor and keep it to yourself. Say things like, "Mmm!" and "Delicious!" when sampling her dishes if you actually want to get laid.

Also, if you want to really impress women, have a couple of things that you can cook well. Nothing is sexier than being fed by a guy who knows how to flavor his food. In college a new guy I was seeing once asked me if I wanted to come by for pasta. I was dreading the meal, figuring it would be spaghetti with some gross Ragu dumped on top of it, but it ended up being fantastic: rigatoni with sausage and peas and sautéed garlic. He even had a little wedge of fresh Parmesan on a plate and a tiny grater. He grated the cheese over my plate like we were in a fancy restaurant.

Something about it was so impressive that I had sex with him.

Chapter Four

The Truth about Dirty Girls and Their Friends

I've Seen a Picture of My Best Friend's Boyfriend's Wiener

I once had a bad fight with a guy I had just started dating. When I said I was leaving to go meet my girlfriend instead of dealing with him being a total bitch to me, he suddenly accused me of loving my best friend more than I loved him. It was such an absurd accusation, and I told him as much, but at the same time, we both knew he was right.

I loved him, but it was a different kind of love from the one I have for my girlfriends. With him, we could do all sorts of awesome things together like kiss on the mouth with tongue and spend the night in the same bed naked (though there was that one time my friend and I woke up in her bed with me in nothing but underpants and her in nothing but tube socks, but we had just passed out drunk—nothing salacious was going on).

Not much can compare to the love I have for men, but nothing can match the closeness that women have with their female compatriots. We tell each other *everything*.

The Straight Dope

I think about what life would be like if I had no girls to gossip with on a regular basis about everything from why I hate my boss today to asking whether it's weird to wear a cream-colored dress to a wedding. They are always there with a straight and solid answer, an answer that's not just rattled off as an afterthought, like it is with a lot of guys. And it's not just the mundane—we can talk about everything from money and work to our futures and deaths. Comments from my girls are thought out, interesting, and funny. Best of all, my girls actually seem to give a shit about discussing the most inane things that would drive even the most sensitive guy crazy.

My boyfriend is *kinda somewhat* sensitive. Sometimes. He has probably cried when his favorite team lost a football game, and he coos like a little girl at pictures of baby monkeys and kitten videos. But every morning when I need some kind of outfit reassurance before facing the world for the day, he inevitably lets me down. These are the times I wish I had a girl around.

Our conversations usually go somewhat like this:

"Is it weird to wear a minidress when I have a fancy PR lunch with some old people at the Carlyle today?"

"Huh?"

"I said, do you think this dress is too short to wear to a meeting? The clients are kind of on the old side."

"No. I don't know. What do you think?" (I think it is. I change.)

"Why did you change? I thought you looked good in that dress."

Recently I came out wearing an olive-green shirt-dress with black tights and black high-heeled boots. It seemed cute as I was putting it on, but on my way out the door I glimpsed at myself in the mirror and realized I kind of looked like a slutty military nurse.

"Hey, do I look like a slutty World War II nurse?"

"Huh?"

"I feel like I look like I'm in some period porn piece and am about to have sex with all the wounded soldiers I've been tending to. Do I? Am I a character in *Saving Ryan's Privates*?"

"No. What? I don't know. What do you think?"

I decide it's fine, mainly because I don't have a good second opinion. Of course, later when I met my friends for happy hour, one of them immediately said, "Nice sexy nurse outfit."

Why Girl Haters Suck

One night I met a guy I was dating at a bar. We hadn't been dating long, and he brought his friend Ben with him, and Ben brought a woman. She was obviously very into Ben. Soon after I arrived she took me aside and probed me for insider information: "How long has he been single? Is he a player? Am I wasting my time?" I didn't really know him that well, so instead I talked to her at length about where she was from and what she did, and I fed her a couple lines about how he was a really nice guy and I thought they'd make a really cute couple.

"I like you!" she suddenly declared out of nowhere, seriously drunk.

"I like you too!" I said. And I did. I always admire a woman who likes her drink, although I thought she was a little too obsessed with this guy whom she'd only hung out with once before.

"No, but I mean, this is different, because I hate girls," she said.

Oh, good God. I was stuck talking with a girl hater! Ironically, I hate girls like that! Why are so many women self-declared girl haters?

Ben's date said, "Yeah, I'm totally a guy's girl. I think girls suck—they're all usually so vapid and lame. I like to drink whiskey with the bros. You're like the only new girl I've ever met that I liked. Hey, dude! I like this girl. You should hold on to her! She's actually a cool chick!" she called out to my new boyfriend. I rolled my eyes.

She was not the first woman to declare to me that she hated girls—or that she was a guy's girl. Those proclamations drive me crazy. What do they even mean? That the girl likes sports? That she can drink a lot? That she has a dirty mouth and says what she means? Most of the women I know are like that, except for maybe the sports thing—but I have seen some frightening, foul-mouthed broads at Yankee Stadium.

The reality is that the woman with no good girlfriends is doomed. The woman who thinks that girls suck just sees all other women as threats to her potential relationships with hot guys, and that's too bad. When and if she lands that hot guy and later decides he's a tool bag and dumps him, who the hell is she going to talk shit about him with at brunch? It's a lonely existence out there for girl haters.

I wish girl haters would stop seeing other women as their competitors. Other women are really their allies. And men should be very wary of girl haters. A woman who has no friends is ten times more likely to be jealous of a guy's daily interactions with other women, even including the old nurse who sticks a thermometer in his bum at the hospital.

"Who does that bitch think she is?" she'll cry. "Did you flirt with her? Did it feel good? You cheating bastard!" And if he does end up a cheating bastard, well, guess who gets the blame. That skank of another woman. "This is why I hate girls!" she'll cry, to nobody at all. She has no friends.

What Women and Their Friends Talk About

Women can talk about anything and everything. I was once accused of hanging out with one friend just because we liked to get hammered and smoke cigarettes. This was true, of course, but we talked a lot while we did so. We talked about work and about our career insecurities, and we boosted each other's egos, telling each other how great we were at our jobs. We came up with clever schemes and business ventures, like Port-o-Patties, pink portable toilets for women with mirrors and hooks on the backs of the doors that would never be out of toilet paper. Women would pay a dollar to use them over regular nasty johns. Of course, by the sober light of day we'd decide we didn't really want to get into the waste management business.

I also spend hours talking about family with my girlfriends, dissecting all the dysfunctional relationships we have with our co-workers or parents or siblings. Then we'll convince each other that we are actually really lucky to have families—most of the time. Sometimes your friends are closer to you than your real family—they can objectively tell you that maybe your mom does favor your other sister, but who cares? You could have been born an orphan without legs.

Still, as most women know, many of our conversations revolve around our relationships with significant others. I hate to say it, but we do spend an inordinate amount of time talking about boys.

What I Know about My Friends' Boyfriends

What do I know about my friends' boyfriends? Too much.

I know far, far too much about the people my friends are dating, and I'm not talking about his sweet gesture the other night or how adorable it was that he planned a foie gras tour of New York City for her birthday. Sure, I know all about that, but I also know that they had sex only twice on a two-week trip to Africa. I know that he likes it when you stick a pinky in his ass, and I know the precise shape, width, and length of his dick. His girlfriend has painted a very graphic picture of it to me, if I haven't already seen a photo. Far too often, this is a typical girls'-night-out conversation:

"So, what's the sex like?"

"He has an awesome dick. I thought that [name

of ex-boyfriend]'s was pretty big, and now I realize he was puny. I've never seen anything like it! I'm almost scared to have sex with him. It's like a Coke can."

"Holy shit! Lucky bitch."

"Yeah, hold on, let me show you a photo."

"Damn, you weren't kidding. I hate you."

I can't tell you how many photos of strange penises I have seen in my life. Since smart phones, web cams, and digital cameras became popular, it's a trend for women to snap photos of wieners and show them off during happy hour. In fact, it was happening so often for a while that I had to ask if I was about to see dick when a friend would say she wanted to show me something. "Relax," she might say. "I'm giving him a blow job, but you can't actually see anything dirty."

Let's Talk about Sex

I know it's not new information that women talk to each other about sex, but sometimes I think it's all I hear about when I'm out with my friends. The following are some recent real conversations I've had.

Conversation 1

"Hey Gillian, do you want to go to 2A for Jenny's birthday drinks?"

"Sure. Did I ever tell you I once had sex in those bathrooms?"

"So funny, I did too!"

Conversation 2

"Should I apply for a position at this other magazine if the money is better but the title is lower?"

"Yeah, go for it. Oh my God, did I tell you Jackie told me that she hasn't had sex in an entire month?"

"What, with her husband?"

"Yeah, she's thinking of having a fling with some guy who works at the café downstairs from her. He's got dreads. Apparently she's always had a thing for rastas."

"Ha ha. Rastas."

Conversation 3

"So not to be TMI, but last night Sam went down on me and it was the best I've ever had in my life."

"Boy Sam or girl Sam?"

"Girl Sam. I spent the night."

"Oh, sweet. Are you guys a couple now?"

"I don't know. She's says she's not ready for a relationship. But I really want to fuck her all the time."

"So what happened with boy Sam?"

"Oh, he still sends me dirty texts all day long. I don't think I can sleep with him—he dated porn stars when he lived in LA. I think he has a dirty dick."

"Yeah, the last thing you need is crabs."

"Totes."

Conversation 4

"Did you hear Joe had sex with Julie last week?"

"Oh my God, we have to tell Alison."

"I think they were broken up at the time."

"Still, that's fucked up."

"No, what's fucked up is Julie now thinks Joe's in love with her and always has been, and she's threatening to tell Alison."

"Dude. This is so twisted. He's so not in love with Julie. Is she really going to tell Alison? And is it so wrong that I can't wait to see how this all turns out?"

"No, we're all pretty excited."

Our Platonic Friends

One of the most memorable lines in *When Harry Met Sally* is "Women and men can never be friends." Women across the country have protested: "Of course we can! Jeff from work is one of my best friends in the city! We're totally platonic besties!" But I think we all know deep down that unless Jeff is seriously deformed, he is potential hook-up material somewhere down the road if things don't work out with our boyfriends—or with Jeff's wife. Of course, this isn't always true, but that's mainly only if the guy is seriously ugly.

The thing that keeps most women from actually hooking up with their best straight guy friend, if he's single, is the fear that things will be ruined, and we'd hate to see something awkward happen with our work bestie. Let's face it, once you let someone stick their peen in your pooter, it's a lot harder to giggle over your co-worker's homemade-hummus obsession or take innocent coffee breaks together. If you do take things a step too far with your work bestie, you'll probably begin to feel a little nervous and maybe start wondering whether he likes you. Or maybe he'll suddenly be all up in your grill, asking if you want to have drinks after work to talk about it.

Women's best platonic guy friend is *kind of* someone we mentally keep on the back burner if the stars were aligned just so, but for the most part, he's not really a direct threat. We've all tried it at some point and quickly discovered how it wasn't meant to be. Of course, there are exceptions to the rule, and sometimes the guy of your dreams turns out to be your platonic best friend—like in shitty Jennifer Garner movies. The one time I thought I was falling in love with my best platonic guy friend and started sleeping with him, he came back from a trip abroad, took me out for martinis, and told me he'd "met somebody awesome." Then he asked me to help him buy lingerie for her, which I dutifully did because I was his best friend and was too mortified to tell him I'd hoped he'd be in love with me instead. Dick.

Friends with Benefits

I once did a *Maxim* column about friends with benefits and the general consensus among women was that friends with benefits is like taking on a complicated home repair project to save money—a good idea in theory, but it hardly ever works out. Unfortunately, women are hardwired to start developing feelings for someone after sex the second time, even if the guy's a toad. I don't know what it is, some cruel biological prank Mother Nature has played on us, probably has some deep-rooted meaning tied to procreation. But you know when you see couples on the street where the woman is twenty times more genetically blessed than the man? She's just had good sex with him a few times. It's that easy for the ugly guys! It's just not really fair.

HAVE YOUR MAN READ THIS, PLEASE: WHY GUYS SHOULD BE AFRAID OF FEMALE BESTIES

Don't all men have that perpetually single former wingman who likes to tell them how much they are missing out on when they're in a relationship? Single women have the equivalent. No matter how settled we are, some buddy will always act like it's better on the other side or convince us that we can do better.

When I was in a long-term relationship that wasn't going so well, I became fast friends with a girl from work who lived in my neighborhood and was in a long-term relationship that wasn't going so well. We'd take the train home together and linger at the station talking until one of us would suggest a quick drink before going home to face our not-going-so-well relationships. This usually turned into two drinks—and we'd moan about our situations and what we were going to do with our lives, which usually turned into both of us getting in trouble with our boyfriends when we came home an hour late smelling like wine. I'd tell my friend my woes, and she'd say things like,

"You know, you can really be doing better. I mean do you want to have a kid with this guy who plays video games all day long instead of looking for a new job?" She was right, and those were the words I wanted to hear. That's what girlfriends do.

And I told her, "And you know, it is kind of weird that your boyfriend stays out with his boss and his boss's girlfriend doing coke until three in the morning on weeknights. It seems like some sort of freaky swingers thing."

And so we encouraged each other to end our relationships, which wasn't easy. A year and a half later, we had some drinks and toasted each other to a job well done.

"Thank God you told me I could do better," I told her, raising my glass and feeling happy I was in a more secure and interesting relationship with someone much more my speed.

"And thank God you reminded me what a bitchy wimp the ex was when I wanted to get back together with him," she said. "If I'd stayed with him, I'd probably never have realized I'm actually a lesbian."

"Cheers to that."

"Cheers."

The point is that, if a woman is feeling iffy about you or thinking you might not be supportive enough, kind enough, or want to have sex enough, she's going to spill everything to her girlfriend, who will tell her that she can do much better than you. So if you suspect someone has put it in her head that she should dump you and move on, you'd be right to suspect her best friend. And if her best friend is single? She might encourage it even if the relationship is swell just because she's bored and wants someone to hit the town with. Watch out. Women can be pretty ruthless.

Chapter Five

Lies We Tell Men

You Were the Best I Ever Had, and I've Only Slept with Nine People

It's my belief that all women are very, very good liars.

Throughout history, women have been told that men are the liars, stinkers, and cheaters. There are cautionary tales about the scumbags who have secret lives with other women, and we are supposed to just accept that men are hardwired bastards who bamboozle their women and that everything out of their mouths is a foul lie. ("We are having the worst time in Vegas, I swear baby. All it does is make me realize how happy I am to have had a comfortable, monogamous relationship with you for eight years! Plus, I'm totally over the drinking and drugs thing.")

Men are made of puppy dog tails and snails and

burning bags of shit. Women, however, are sweet, sugary, and everything nice. They don't cheat, and they certainly don't lie. Good God. That is a total lie in and of itself.

Women are positively *ruthless* when it comes to stretching the truth. I've heard (and sometimes told) some serious whoppers in my life, and the ease and impressive theatrics of these lies are pretty astounding. I think the reason women can get away with bullshitting is because no one suspects us of bullshitting. In that regard, it's pretty awesome being a woman. I've actually heard a man tell me that he doesn't think women ever cheat or lie. That's how good we are at it. They don't suspect a *thing*.

The Number-One Lie We Tell Our Boyfriends

There comes a time in every new relationship, a time that women dread and fear more than anything. No, it's not the first time we have sex. And it's not "Have you been tested?" No, the most dreaded moment in the new relationship is when the guy asks how many people we've had sex with. I guarantee that 95 percent of the time, the answer is a big, fat, juicy lie.

A good friend of mine has had sex with about forty guys. She's thirty and likes to party and have sex. Nothing wrong with that—the numbers just racked up after a lot of alcohol and dancing and meeting cute, sweaty boys in crowded bars and house parties, and she liked to keep the party going back at her apartment. She always used condoms and was happy to see the dudes go in the morning so she didn't suffer from a slut complex or feel like she was being used. It was always her choice. But still, she felt ashamed at having so many notches on her belt, and there was no way in hell she would ever tell a guy she'd been with that many dudes. I asked her what she told her boyfriend when they had "the talk." "Nine," she said.

Ah yes, nine. The magic number. It's high enough to be believable but doesn't hit the double digits, which really freaks men out. I know a lot of women who have said nine, myself included.

"What am I going to say, I've had sex with forty guys, most of them veritable strangers?" she said. "That's not going to fly! I'm pretty positive I'll never tell any guy the truth, not even the person I'll spend the rest of my life with."

Wise move. Why should we be honest about

this? We all know that guys can fuck as many people as they want and it's not a big deal and that women must remain chaste and not sleep with more than nine people or they're gross whores. But guys are crazy to think that we haven't had sex with many people before them. Who do they think they're having all of those one-night stands with? Girls who also have only nine partners?

When I wrote a *Maxim* column on the subject, I asked my then-boyfriend what he thought of women who had a high number of partners. He and I had never actually had "the talk," mainly because neither of us ever instigated it. I didn't want to know if he'd slept with eighty chicks, and he didn't need to know that I once added a veritable stranger to my roster during at a music festival.

"So what do you think is a high number for girls?" I asked him casually, as we were walking around his neighborhood, holding hands and trying to decide where to have lunch.

"I mean, I guess anything above…" he started.

I held my breath. "Say thirty!" I silently willed. "Something high!"

"Twelve."

"Twelve?" I asked him. "Do you really think that's high?" He glanced at me. I looked away, guiltily.

"Yeah, that's really high!" he said. "You don't think so?"

"Um, I think something more like twenty or thirty is high," I said, waiting for his reaction. I got it in the form of mock retching on the sidewalk.

"Twenty! Disgusting!" he cried. "Who is having sex with twenty different guys? That's seriously slutty. Ew."

Damn it. I'd always suspected, and now it was confirmed that I was seriously slutty.

"But if a woman has been having sex since she was sixteen and is now twenty-eight, then that means she's averaging only two mates a year! What about college when girls have lots of sex with…"

"Sixteen? Who is having sex at sixteen and then having two partners a year?" Oh dear. My enlightened boyfriend, as it turned out, knew nothing about women.

"Oh, I don't know," I said. "Total sluts, I guess. But it doesn't matter because my number isn't nearly that high. I've just had lots of boyfriends, so I'm lucky I've been able to keep it really low. I'm not even in the double digits! But let's not talk about us. Anyway, do you want to go get Mexican for lunch? I'm craving tacos and margaritas. Mmm, doesn't that sound good?" I said, giving him a kiss on the cheek and not feeling remotely ashamed about the fact that I'd just told the man I loved a big fat, blatant lie.

Believing in the Lie

A good friend of mine is a compulsive liar when it comes to her boyfriends. She says it started when she was dating a jealous control freak who'd get mad at her if she was doing something as innocent as watching *Top Chef* and drinking wine at a friend's place with another guy in the room. And so she started omitting details that she thought would make him jealous. No harm done, right? Except soon it became her habit to lie about every single thing to the men she dated, even though none of them were psycho, jealous freaks like the first guy. That one sad man's jealousy had actually turned her into the lying freak.

"Last night I was at work a little late and my boyfriend called and then he asked if anyone was still at work with me and I automatically said no," she said, adding that one of her male co-workers was actually there. "I don't know why I didn't tell him. There's nothing going on whatsoever between me and the guy; he's like forty and overweight and unattractive. I'm just used to lying about stuff like that."

As I said, the ease with which little white lies roll off the tongue for most women is astounding. A friend of mine likes to call it "believing in the lie."

"You just have to believe in it," she told me once, when I was practicing what I was going to say to a guy I was dating after I didn't call him or go to his place like I'd promised I would. The reason I didn't call him or go to his place was because I'd downed a bunch of dirty martinis, ended up stripping during amateur night at a seedy club, and then spent the night on the couch of a co-worker's house, and I might have also made out with him a little bit.

After drinking way too much one night out in college, I'd gone with a few girlfriends to this really sad, empty strip place in North Beach in San Francisco, and they'd dared me to go onstage and strip. It was amateur night, hardly anyone was there, and they were playing Prince, so I took the dare. My friends call it the peekaboo night, since I was wearing one of those childish bras that flat people wear that snap in the front, and I'd opened it and given a little peekaboo to the audience with each boob (the audience of two old men, a bored bartender, and two hysterical girlfriends). But I digress. The next day, I awoke facedown on a strange pleather couch with a serious vodka hangover and horrible flashbacks running through my head—stripping, making out with a co-worker, not calling my boyfriend, and holy fuck is it two in the afternoon—I immediately called my best friend to tell her the horrifying situation.

"Meet me now," she said. "Do not call your boyfriend until we hash out what you're going to say first." I agreed. I was in no state to make any clear judgments or good excuses. And by the light of day, I could see that the co-worker was in nothing but his boxers passed out at the other end of the couch. Shit, shit, shit—what had I done?

When I met my friend at a coffee shop near her work, the first thing she did was mime the peekaboo bra act for me and start cracking up.

"Bitch, no. I seriously can't think about that. I am so embarrassed I am going to die," I said.

"Oh, no, you probably don't even remember the worst part," she said. "When the song was done, the bar was closing so the house lights came up. You'd flung your clothes into the audience during the striptease so you were just standing there in harsh light in your flowery underpants, covering your boobs with your arms," she said, laughing harder. "We had to bring your clothes to the stage for you!"

"Shut up!" I wailed. "Help me! What am I going to tell Eric?"

"OK, here's the plan," she said. "Tell him we all got seriously wasted and went back to Jessie's to hang out. I had your phone in my purse and suddenly left to meet Cody without saying anything to you guys because he and I were fighting. You ended up passing out at Jessie's and didn't wake up until twelve and realized you didn't have your phone. Jessie was at work, and you had no way to get in touch with anyone until you walked to my work and picked up the phone because you don't know his number by heart. Got it?"

"He's going to know it's a lie!" I wailed. I am not the world's best liar. I get really uncomfortable and red-faced and feel like it's pretty obvious I'm spinning yarns. Also, I don't know how to keep complicated stories like that straight. It's always generally been better to try to tell the sort-of truth for me, but I didn't want to let a single moment from the night before slip. This had been a really bad one.

"Gillian," she said. "Believe this was the case. Do not believe that last night you got up and peekabooed your titties at an amateur strip club and then called your gross co-worker to make out even though we told you not to!" She couldn't help but smile again at the memory. "Seriously, what happened last night was we all went to Jessie's, you blacked out from drinking too much, woke up super late to no phone and no one else at her place. End of story. So you got hammered and never called or showed up. Shit happens. It doesn't mean you did anything bad."

"You're right," I said. 'I didn't do anything bad! I was just hanging with you girls and got too messed up to call or even think straight."

Believe in the lie.

A vision of an old man in a hat pulled low, throwing a single dollar on the stage while my naked body boogied flashed through my head. Ick, no. Jessie's apartment. We all went to Jessie's apartment.

I was ready to call my boyfriend and explain.

My girlfriend promised to stand right by me. I was shaking as I dialed his number, and his voice was stony when he answered.

"Oh my God, I am so sorry," I started. "I feel so terrible. I blacked out at Jessie's and didn't have my phone..." I went on to explain what had happened, totally nervous that he could smell the lie but certainly unable to tell him the truth. He demanded to know why I hadn't just called earlier at midnight when I said I would tell him where to meet me. I froze. I had no excuse. My friend realized I was stuttering and grabbed the phone out of my hand.

"Hey, Eric, I am so sorry I had Gill's phone last night," she said. "Yeah, we were hammered, Gill blacked out, and I left Jessie's not knowing I had it with me. OK, see you later!" she chirped, handing the phone back to me. He was more relaxed now and agreed to meet me for a drink later in the evening so I could redeem myself.

"See, that was easy," my friend said, dialing another number on her phone. "Hey, Jessie?" she said into the receiver. "If Eric asks you, last night Gill blacked out at your place. I know! Me too! I will never, for as long as I live, forget that peekaboo thing. Ha ha ha yeah, peekabooby! Oh my God, I'm dying!" she said, doubling over in laughter again as I hung my head in my hands and yearned, not for the first time, for a time machine.

Believe in the lie. I'd have to continue to believe it that night and until the end of that relationship so I'd never slip up.

End of story? The boyfriend and I broke up a few weeks later, when I realized that I wasn't the best girlfriend if I was doing things like that. I rebound dated the co-worker briefly, until he caught me making out in the bathroom with a girl at a lesbian bar my sister had dragged me to. What can I say, I was in my early twenties. Being totally shameless at the time was part of my lifestyle.

Lies We Tell in the Sack

It's not so much a lie that we tell in the sack. It's called faking it. As women, we know faking it is stupid and essentially robs us of our own pleasure, but sometimes the guy is just not going to give us that pleasure, and frankly we need a way to get him off our backs—or whatever position we're in at the time.

I really don't bother with faking anymore, but

back when I was in my early twenties, I dated a guy with whom I basically forged it for two full years. I'm ashamed to admit it, but he just wasn't aware of the clit and I was too shy to explain it to him. Plus, I stupidly faked it early on, and he thought I could come from about thirty seconds of pumping away. It was my fault really. Luckily, because we went out drinking a lot, we had a lot of morning sex instead of night sex since we'd often pass out in the evening. I had a mini vibrator stashed in my guest drawer, and when he'd go to the shower, I'd rush out and sneakily use it, one eye on the door in case he came out of the bathroom, and a pillow over my lap to drown out the noise so I'd at least get some sort of satisfaction from our sexual encounters, even if he wasn't actually in the room when I got off. I never told him until we broke up for good, because I found out he'd been cheating on me. With both women *and* men.

Some Dirty Girls tend to still fake it all the time, even though what they are doing is simply a disservice to other women. If you need to teach and guide a guy on how to get you off, just do it. Even if it doesn't work out with him, be nice and prep him for the next chick. Nothing is lamer than a guy who doesn't care how to pleasure a girl because he's never had to, because someone writhed and screamed like a banshee a mere twenty seconds into it. Yes, there is that mythical woman who can come just from sex almost immediately, but I've never met her, and I've met a lot of women. Most every woman I know needs someone to go down on her, manual stimulation, to be on top and positioned just right, or to use a vibrator at the same time to get off during sex. Lying on your back for some rocking missionary does feel awesome, but it very rarely hits the right spot just so.

Lies We Tell Our Friends

Women, like men, sometimes lie to other women about how often they're getting laid and how good it is. Women like to keep up appearances, and one thing they like to put a fake front on is their sex lives. If we're with a group of girls and one is talking about how she enjoys sex with her boyfriend almost every night, the other women will instantly lie about how often they're doing it so it doesn't sound like they have lame sex lives in comparison. This isn't the case between very close friends—they would never lie about something like this, but casual acquaintances definitely like to keep up with the Joneses, sexually.

I once had a friend who was having serious sex with a guy she was dating, and we all had to endure listening to her erotic tales at brunch, even though the rest of us were either single or in boring relationships. It annoyed us to no end.

"Oh my God, you guys, last night we broke the bed we were fucking so hard," she said one morning. I caught the glance of another girl, and we automatically rolled our eyes. Great—she may as well have told us that she was making $100,000 more than us a year.

"Wow, what happened?" we all asked, unenthusiastically.

"We were having sex for hours when we got home, and we were trying all these crazy positions and I was holding on to the bed frame at one point and we were doing it so hard that the headboard came off in my hands!" she said. "You should see my bruises!"

Later I'd purposely walk home with someone else to dissect this.

"I mean, it sounds fun and all, but would you really want to have sex for hours? I feel like I would be all chafed and just give up and go to sleep after sixty minutes," I'd say, trying not to sound bitter.

"Yeah, I don't want to break my bed; I just got it from Crate and Barrel. What a waste!" she'd say.

"And bruises? Yuck!"

"Ew, yeah, gross!"

The next weekend, it was the same deal.

"His dick, I'm telling you, it's huge. It hurts me. I don't know what to do with it sometimes," our friend would say.

"How many times did you do it last night?" we'd ask, annoyed but still kind of curious.

"I don't even know, at least three," she'd say. "It's amazing that he is always ready to go for round two."

When she'd go to the bathroom, someone would always say, "I am so sick of hearing about this!" and we'd all collectively agree, jealous she was having such good sex all the time with a giant penis and we weren't.

Well, a few years later, this friend suddenly met someone new, and they had a whirlwind affair and got engaged early on in the relationship. I met her for drinks to hear all about him and the new development.

"It's the most amazing sex," she told me. "I've never felt anything like it. It's like, lightning bolts."

"But what about your ex?" I asked. "You said you had the best sex with him."

"Ugh, no, I don't think I ever even came once with him," she said. "He hated going down on me and I don't think he did it ever, and a lot of times he was so wasted he had a hard time getting it up."

"Ohhh…" I said, both confused and secretly gleeful I'd caught her in a lie. Years later! I told her I hoped she'd be really happy with the new guy, and on the walk home, I immediately called the other brunch pal. "You're never gonna guess what I just found out," I said.

Oh, man, did it make us happy. But it also reiterated what I already knew to be true. When women go on about how awesome their sex life is to other women, something is fishy. If you have an amazing sex life, you spend more time humping than bragging about it. And most of my friends, the honest ones, are much more likely to tell me that they either want it more than their boyfriends give and they're getting depressed about it or that they're happy to hump once a week.

"That's enough for me," one friend recently

told me. "What can I say, I'm just not that horny anymore." At least I totally believe her. No one is going to lie about suddenly becoming frigid.

Rejection Lies

Women, for the most part, try to be pretty nice when it comes to rejecting guys they have no interest in. Of course, we do pull shit like giving a fake phone number or just never contacting them again when we don't want to deal. Overall, though, I think we have a more tactful approach to dismissing men than they do with us. Of course, some rejection lies are the exact same with both sexes. Especially the typical "I just need some alone time."

As far as I know, "I just need some time to figure out who I am, I'm not sure what I want, I'm just really confused right now, blah, blah, blah" is code for "I've met someone that I'm either already fucking or desperate to have sex with and you're standing in the way." The truth hurts. But most people in relationships don't suddenly get "confused about who they are." They are bored and want to have sex or at least a new emotional love affair with someone new. We're led to believe that mainly men pull this shit, but I know a bunch of girls who have used this line too. I have to admit, I even used it once. Although I added "I really think I need to be alone right now so I can figure out what it is I want, I'm confused about who I am and what I am doing in life, and it's just a trial separation—I just need a little space to clear my head and be alone." Alone. Yeesh—I actually feel bad for being such a turd. I didn't exactly have someone new lined up in the wings, but I did have someone I made out with a bit regularly for the couple of months that followed the breakup. It eased the transition, something that most people, especially women seem to need.

So it's annoying when men break up with us out of the blue—we haven't had time to line up our breakup makeout partner and are 100 percent alone. Not fair! Rejection is ugly.

A Cautionary Tale

When I was in college, my best friend and I went to a Halloween costume party. She was dressed as a dead Elizabethan woman with her head chopped off. She'd borrowed an elaborate dress from a friend who worked for the San Francisco Opera, and she looked amazing, with white makeup and a big gaping wound around her neck with blood dripping out. I was dressed as a tranny. Yes, a tranny. I'd wanted to go as a hunchbacked hooker, but my friend refused to go out with me if I would be stooped over with a gigantic hunchback attached to my shoulders. I thought it was funny, but in the end, she won. I was still wearing the hooker outfit though and knew I couldn't just go out as a big slut. So I added a five-o'clock shadow to my face and dark lip liner to my lips, and I stuffed my pants with two tennis balls so I had a big bulge in my tight miniskirt. My friend shook her head at me: "You're a serious freak."

"Do you want me to add the hunchback again?" I asked her. She didn't. We made our way to the party and proceeded to drink heavily. Once there, someone we knew offered us a half hit of ecstasy, which we split. Everything was fun, and I was feeling fine and laughing as people came up and asked if I was a man or a woman.

When a guy dressed up as Andy Warhol came up and started chatting with me, I was more than happy to gab away. I had no idea whether he was cute, but he suddenly asked, "Hey, what did you do last night by any chance?" I'd actually gone to a Fatboy Slim concert. Normally I probably would have just told this dude that I'd gone to a concert, but I was feeling happy and funny, so I decided to tell him the whole story.

"Oh my God, well, I went to this stupid-ass Fatboy Slim concert with this girl I work with who I don't even like all that much, and she brought this random dude to set me up with and he turned out to be a big loser and the whole event was a nightmare. He was not cute, he was boring, and at one point he dumped his entire pint of beer in my lap. It was awful. I actually pulled the slip and told them I was going to the bathroom and hopped in a cab to get the hell out of there. I told the chick I was sick, but I just had to get away from that fucking dork." I was laughing as I told the story, sure Andy Warhol would think this was funny too. He looked a little confused. "Anyway, what did you do last night?" I asked, feeling cute and flirty.

"Um, I was at the Fatboy Slim concert too," he said.

"No way! How funny! Where were you standing?" I asked him.

"Well, I was sitting actually," he said. "There are those tables for four behind the standing room?"

"That's where I was! We were to the left of the stage. Where were you?" I asked.

"Yeah, I was left of stage too," he said.

"Weird!" I cried.

"Actually, I was with you."

"What?" I said, confused.

"Yeah. Uh, I'm Jenna's friend? It's me, Alex."

Holy motherfucking love of God. Alex was Andy Warhol. Andy Warhol was last night's lame ass in disguise. I didn't recognize him in the powder wig and big-framed glasses. I'd called him a loser to his face. My heart suddenly felt like a brick falling out of my butt. I froze and felt sick and dizzy. Suddenly my friend Corinne walked by and I grabbed her for support.

"Oh, Corinne, hey, this is Alex. He's Jenna's friend," I yelled at her above the noise and music. She didn't understand what I was saying and yelled back, "Jenna? Ugh, I hate that girl, she bugs!" and went on her merry way. Alex looked at me with hurt behind those goofy Warhol glasses, and I didn't know what else to do: I leaned in and kissed him on the lips. "Wow, I am really messed up tonight! But I need another drink," I said, laughing and dancing backward away from him and toward the bar. I felt awful. I spent the rest of the night looking out for Andy Warhol so I could avoid him, which wasn't easy because there were three of them roaming around. I ended up stuck in conversation with someone else. Toward the end of the night, I felt a tap on my shoulder. Alex was back. I cringed, waiting for him to chew me out for being such a huge horrible bitch.

"You," he said. "You are the most fascinating woman I have ever met. I think I am in love with you." Whoa. This was not what I was expecting.

"Really?" I asked, once again very confused.

"You were so good at pretending you didn't know who I was I actually believed you for a few minutes," he said. "You're hilarious! So, can I get your number?"

"Um, of course!" I said, pretending to be very interested in him too, to make up for the fact that I'd been so painfully cruel when I didn't recognize him. I gave him my number and a few days later met him for coffee out of total guilt. The worst part? When I met him at the café, he was already there, sitting a table away from the one I'd chosen.

"Hey, did you not see me?" he asked, scooting over to my table.

"Oh, I guess not," I said.

The truth was that I'd seen him and looked

right through him. For the life of me I still couldn't remember what he looked like. Poor guy really was actually that boring and unmemorable. After that, I just started ignoring his calls until he finally gave up. It was easier.

HAVE YOUR MAN READ THIS, PLEASE: WHEN YOU CAN RIGHTFULLY SUSPECT YOUR GIRLFRIEND OF LYING

One of the times women lie is when men ask, "Am I the best you have ever had?" and/ or, "Do I have the biggest penis you have ever seen?" Every woman will respond, "Of course." Why would we say, "Well, you're a nice size and all, but I once dated this Brazilian who was packing so much heat he almost split me in two!" If you do not want to be lied to, then do not ask stupid questions.

Women also might lie if you ask whether they've ever cheated on someone. Occasionally, if a woman is having a heart-to-heart with a beau and has decided that complete and utter honesty is the best policy, then she will cop to it, but for the most part, women are aware that admitting this will make men automatically suspicious of them, no matter how loyal and devoted we are. I once made the mistake of telling someone new that I had kissed a bartender behind my ex-boyfriend's back toward the end of the relationship. Can you imagine how many times during arguments he would say things like, "Well, you just want to go and kiss every random bartender you see!" I regretted that one.

Women might also, occasionally, stretch the truth about how late we were out and with whom exactly, if we were doing something we didn't think you would approve of. When I went to Atlantic City for a good friend's birthday, I ended up staying up all night gambling and drinking, and didn't stop throwing $5 chips at the craps table until my friend called and told me it was noon and time to check out of the hotel. I was having an awesome time, and ended up making about three hundred bucks. However, I did not tell my boyfriend this when he asked what time we went to bed—I told him we all passed out around four in the morning, something a bit more respectable than, well, never. It wasn't that I had actually done anything particularly wrong—I wasn't flirting with guys, and another friend was by my side the entire time—but I felt he would disapprove, and I was right. Women will stretch the truth a little bit if they think it will save them from getting into trouble. It probably stems from lying to our mothers about who we'd been with and how we were just holding those cigarettes in our bag for a friend.

Chapter Six

DJ Diddle

The Reality of Women, Masturbation, and Porn

I was about ten when I first saw my parent's *National Geographic* magazines, with images depicting Amazon tribeswomen with dangling oblong boobies and occasionally the exciting peek of peen under a loincloth. I pored over these, pretending to be interested in what was happening around the world when in fact I was simply interested in seeing naked people and how it made me feel. I discussed this at length with other girlfriends in the fifth grade, all of whom had similar thoughts and feelings on the matter.

"It makes me feel funny down there," I'd say, referring to a sex scene I'd caught in an R-rated movie the night before.

"It makes my pee pee go boom boom," said one, in what might be the most accurate description of being horny I have ever heard in my life.

But at the time, I just looked at images when and where I could. I didn't touch myself anywhere. I wouldn't have known what to do anyway. But a few years later, when I was about fourteen, my sister pointed out the clitoris on a diagram in her biology book and informed me that *that* was what made sex feel good.

"When women touch it, it supposedly feels amazing," she said. "But don't tell mom or anyone else I showed you this." Thank God for older sisters. This one changed my world for good.

Women Who Love Themselves

Asking the question "Do women masturbate?" is like asking "Do back and foot rubs feel nice?" Hell. Yes. The first column I did for *Maxim* was about just how much Dirty Girls masturbate. Every single woman I spoke with not only copped to doing it but also copped to doing it all the time—and some copped to doing it at least once a day. Some women admitted that, on occasion, they did it even more than that.

"Women masturbate *that* much?" a guy friend asked me when I mentioned it.

"As much as you do, dude," I assured him.

"That's like, once or twice a week, I guess?"

"Oh, then, never mind. Most women masturbate more than you do."

The average amount most women devoted to self-love was roughly twice a week, but it was much, much higher for single women.

"I usually do it twice a day," said Doree, a single twenty-six-year-old in ad sales who lives alone. "I do it when I get out of the shower and am still naked, before I get dressed and ready for work, and then I do it every night before I go to sleep." A lot of the single women talked about doing it almost every single night, because why the hell not? "It puts me to sleep," said one woman. And another, a thirty-year-old in public relations, said she did it once a night before she went to bed and sometimes all morning long on weekends.

"I don't really have to be up and anywhere until I'm meeting friends for brunch, so I'll lay around in bed and do it a couple times on Saturday and Sunday mornings," she said. "The other day I did it five times. I'd just wait a few minutes between each session, or watch another *Scrubs* rerun and then go at it again."

Even the women in relationships, and surprisingly, the ones who lived with their partners, still said they did it a few times a week.

"Generally I do it when my boyfriend is making breakfast and I'm in the shower," said one woman, who likes to use the detachable showerhead that she specifically installed in their bathroom. "It depends on how rushed I am, but it's certainly at least twice a week."

"I like to actually use my vibrator a lot with my boyfriend, but I still use it when he's not around. If he goes to work first, or he has to do something after work, I go for it. I really just seize any opportunity I can," said Wendy, a journalist friend of mine. "It's so quick, and I don't even have to get naked. Just some quick over the pants action with my trusty pocket rocket and a dirty website and bam, done."

Another pal said she did it every time she had the opportunity. "A lot of times I'm between TV shows and have a couple minutes to kill, and the boyfriend isn't home. It just takes a minute. Sometimes less, depending on what I'm looking at and how long or short I want the session to last."

I asked her what she meant by that, and she explained that usually she does it because it's super quick, always happens, and is a fast feel-good pick-me-up, but other times she really gets into it and takes her time looking at various images and videos, uses more than one toy, whips out the lube, and so on. "Those are the much rarer special moments," she said. "I usually need to know I have plenty of time. And even then I need to stop myself from getting off too quickly. Sometimes using a vibe, it happens too soon and I get bummed. I'm my own preemie ejaculator. It's like having bad sex with a college kid, except I'm in charge."

Devices Women Use

I got an IM recently from a friend of mine, saying "I want this sex toy like *whoa*." I clicked on the link, and it showed a somewhat scary-looking device that resembled a wheel with ten pink rubber tongues sticking out of it. Press the button and the wheel whirred in circles, making the tongues flick the right spot. It did look pretty awesome.

"Wow," I wrote back. "I need something new too. I've had the same trusty pocket rocket for five years," I said.

"Yeah, but that works," she answered. "I once tested that Jimmy Jane $350 one for a magazine article, and it worked just like the pocket rocket. I mean what does a $350 orgasm feel like? The same as all the others!"

"True," I said, though I was still thinking that the wheeled device might be worth the $55 splurge.

Ah, vibes. Back in the 1870s, "masturbating a woman" was thought to be a cure for hysteria, which, come to think of it, it really is. But a doctor or husband had to perform it, and come on, do you think those husbands knew what they were doing? It's still not easy to get off from a guy rubbing you all over the place down there unless he's really good at it and uses some sort of lube. But all this cumbersome rubbing led to the invention of the steam-powered Manipulator, a vibrating sphere that did the dirty work as the woman laid on a table at her doctor's office. Soon, with the invention of electricity, a whole new batch of electric machines were invented—bought and used freely and happily by ladies. Those machines were in women's homes years before other wonderful time-saving devices like the washing machine and vacuum cleaner. Why was it totally acceptable for women to cure hysteria by squatting on a vibrating block and getting off? Because the men and doctors didn't think it was sexual at all. According to them, sexual pleasure was derived exclusively from inserting things into the vagina. Oh, how we laugh now to think of such things! Though sadly, the same is still true for a lot of dudes today.

Unfortunately, fellas and prudes caught on and the lovely mother's helpers were eventually shunned as evil machines, as was anything that was thought to bring sexual pleasure to women in those dreary times (though you could always find a "neck massager" in catalogs). And here you thought the Sharper Image inventory was a new thing— just imagine, your Grandma Rose was probably investing in neck massagers herself, sneaking in between making quilts and Jell-O molds to quickly and quietly get off when no one was looking. Now, of course, you can get vibrators anywhere and everywhere, and most important, you can buy them online. They arrive at your home two days later, and you don't have to feel embarrassed as you pay for your hot new sex toy.

These orgasm triggers are certainly the most popular way to reach the big O, but not the only way.

"I like to use the electric toothbrush," one girl told me. "I've never had to actually buy a vibrator—I've just been able to get them at Target, and you recharge them at night so there's no concern about running out of batteries." Smart—every single woman I know pilfers batteries from the remote control when the vibrator is running a little low on juice, thus rendering their remote controls useless, which is highly annoying. Of course, not nearly as annoying as running out of power when you're in the middle of a masturbatory session. Men may get blue balls, but women have a similar condition: complete and utter frustration at a dead vibrator. Which, in a sense, is the exact same thing as hysteria.

The toothbrush girl continued to tell me that she doesn't put the bristles directly on her parts to stimulate them but instead used the flat back part.

"Is this the same brush you use on your teeth?" I asked her.

"It is, but I change the heads, depending on whether I'm putting it in my mouth to brush my teeth or down there," she said. "They're color coordinated." Color-coordinated toothbrush heads to masturbate? Believe me, I've heard weirder things.

"I only use the showerhead," said Kelsey, one of the women I interviewed for *Maxim*. "I learned how to do it back in high school when we lived overseas and had detachable showerheads in all our bathrooms, and I've never really used anything else. I've had vibrators, but I'm so used to how the water feels I like it best. I've bought and installed them in all the apartments I've lived in. If I'm in a place that doesn't have a showerhead like my apartment does, then I usually run a bath and kind of scooch down and position myself so I'm right underneath the faucet and go to town."

I asked if she just held it at the right spot and waited for it to work its magic.

"Mostly, but sometimes I twist the showerhead off so it's just like a steady stream, like a small hose instead of a spray going all over the place," she said. "It's easier to control. The one thing you don't want to do is have too strong of water pressure," she said. "If it's coming out to fast or too hard, it actually hurts instead of feeling good, and it will make you feel like you're peeing your pants," she said. "You need to make sure the temperature is perfect too. You can't do this with cold water. You also don't want to get any water up there. Just aim it right at the clit. You're looking for an orgasm, not a douche. And I think it's supposed to be bad for you when you shoot water all up in there."

Water masturbation techniques are almost as old as the steam-powered manipulator, if not older. But hydrotherapy and electronics certainly aren't the only ways women bring themselves to the height of ecstasy when no one else is in the room.

"I hump my pillow," said an old college friend when I asked about various preferred methods of masturbation.

"You what?" I said, never once thinking in all my own years of self-exploration that humping a pillow would be something fun to do.

"Well, it started off as teddy bears when I was a kid," she explained.

"You used to hump your teddy bears?" I asked her.

"Yeah, my teddy bears in bed. I've been doing it since as long as I can remember, I mean even as young as four probably. It always felt good to rub my crotch up against them, and when I outgrew stuffed animals, I turned to my pillow, which basically did the same thing. I just put it between my legs and hump it. Sometimes I mount it." I couldn't stop laughing, mainly because of the word *mount* but also because I thought it was kind of gross to do that to something you lay your head on each night.

"Seriously, it feels good to me. Now I can even do it with humping my hand," she said.

"So you're not actually just touching your clit with a few fingers?" I asked.

"No, it's much more of a rubbing back and forth up against something motion. It's good that I can come this way. It made it easier for me to have an orgasm from sex because if I'm on top, I know how to position myself so that it rubs in the right way."

That shut me up. Most women I know have trouble from having an orgasm from intercourse, and a lot of us blame it on our regular clitoral stimulation from our trusty machines.

I asked if she had any tips on how to get off just from sex, and she said it wasn't just from sex. "I don't really know anyone that gets off just from a peen inside them," she said. "It's about rubbing my entire crotch against his in the right way. If I could do it against my bears, surely I can do it against anything kind of hard and between my legs."

I was suddenly jealous. But this got me to wondering how many women worried that their vibes were making them numb to other sensations. I asked my friends if any of them had given them up for a while.

"I gave up my vibrator for a few months while I experimented with just trying to reach orgasm through sex," said Alison, a friend of mine who was worried that she'd desensitized herself with her Hitachi Magic Wand. "It didn't really help, but I did start enjoying orgasms with him a little bit more. He still had to go down on me for me to reach them, or I had to be on top and directly stimulating myself with my hand, but they seemed a little more intense. Maybe it was all in my head, though."

I've talked to lots of women who say they masturbate so often that they don't understand how a man will ever please them the same way. And it *is* different. Vibrators make you get off so quick and effortlessly, that they can make you feel almost lazy about sex and the whole concept of working toward the goal of that lovely, light-headed feeling that we all enjoy so much. But as with anything that is quick and easy as opposed to something you really have to strive for, it's somehow slightly less satisfying than a good romp in the hay with someone who appreciates your body and wants to touch, kiss, and lick you in all sorts of manners to reduce your hysteria.

It's like eating homemade pie as opposed to a store-bought one. Sure, they are both delicious and satisfy a craving, but you know that homemade pie, with its lard crust and uneven sugary clumps will ultimately be tastier than the Entenmann's off the shelf.

Women and Porn

I once interviewed countless women about their porn-watching habits for a *Maxim* article, and I have to say, what I found wasn't totally surprising. It turns out most women watch it—a lot. They just don't let the men in their lives know exactly how much, and they also get offended when or if they find out their boyfriends have subscriptions to ButtPirates.com, even though they themselves may regularly visit sites that show skinny women getting tag-teamed by big men.

Gina, a twenty-eight-year-old journalist, said she looks at porn almost every day, which also means that she masturbates almost every day. "Is there any other reason to look at this stuff?" I asked. No.

"I discovered a site called XTube.com," she told

me, explaining that it was all sorts of dirty pictures and videos. "I only started going online for porn when it became free on this site. I used to read dirty books because the Internet was lame—you had to pay, or they'd show you a snippet and then try and make you pay. I'm both horny and cheap."

"What about YouPorn?" I asked, having discovered through my research that YouPorn and XTube were the most popular sites for chicks to visit when they're playing DJ Diddles.

"Sometimes I go there too," she says. "But for some reason this one is always my standby. I generally look at regular straight stuff, but I also like to check out the anal."

Ah, yes. Anal, I also discovered, is a very common type of pornography for women. Almost every Dirty Girl I talked to said they usually checked out videos of butt sex and threesomes—because they were things they were interested in doing in fantasy but would never actually do in real life.

"I'm a good Jewish girl!" Rebecca told me when I asked why she liked looking at anal so much. "We don't do things like that! I just fantasize about it."

Another woman told me that she loved watching

videos so much because she wanted to like it and do it because it seemed so sexy and taboo. "We tried lube, I read tips on how to do it, I even asked my gay guy friends," she said. "But my ass is like Charlie and the chocolate factory. No one ever goes in; no one ever comes out."

"Nothing ever comes out?" I said.

"Oh, wait, well, you know. Actually maybe I shouldn't say 'chocolate factory' either. But it just doesn't work! Seriously, it senses penis and seals up so tight you can't get an oiled pinky in there let alone a wiener."

So, many women look at butt sex as the ultimate taboo turn-on for porn, and it seems like just as many look at threesomes. Not at that typical male fantasy of two girls and one guy—most of them looked at porn that showed two or more men with one woman. I asked them why.

"I have a fantasy to have three different guys pleasing me in various ways at once," said Julie, a twenty-seven-year-old waitress. "I just would never know how to go about actually fulfilling it, and at the end of the day, I'm a relationship kind of girl, not a porno girl getting pounded by three dudes at once."

Some women said they also looked at lesbians, because it turned them on and it was something they'd thought about or even done in the past. "It's just sexy," said one girl. "I just have a feeling she would know what she was doing down there, unlike a lot of the guys I've been with who immediately just want to stick it in."

A handful of women confessed they sometimes looked at really weird and twisted stuff. "Gay dudes," said Laura, a twenty-nine-year-old web designer. "I love watching gay guy porn. I don't know why it turns me on so much, but it's the only thing that makes me come. Then when I'm actually with my boyfriend, a lot of times I fantasize that he's getting humped by a guy! If he was *actually* getting humped by a guy I would cry and hate it. So I can't explain why it turns me on in my head. I think it's watching a big dude have to submit. I probably get some sort of sick pleasure out of watching a man be treated like a woman."

Come to think of it, Laura is kind of a tall, bad-ass chick who doesn't take shit from a lot of people. I can totally understand the joy in watching a man have to take it like he's given it so many times before. Also, it combines that other taboo porn topic that the ladies all seem to love so much—buggering up the bum!

The weirdest answer I got from one of the women was a girl who said she had recently gone through a tranny phase. "I liked videos of people having sex with trannies. There are all sorts of weird ones!" she said. "You would think it's all straight men from New Jersey, but there are a bunch with women having sex with trannies! It's really weird." She also said she used to like to watch stuff that she really felt bad about later, like women getting *bukkaked* (that's when a group of guys openly splooge on a woman's face—I am sorry I had to be the one to explain that and I hope you aren't eating breakfast). "It's terribly degrading toward women, but for some reason it turned me on," she said. "I don't know what my issues are, but I love porn and I like a whole lot of creepy variety."

Several women said they really wished they could admit to their partners how much they enjoyed looking at it and what they liked to watch but they didn't want to be judged by them.

"I think it would be so great if I could whip open the computer on the bed at night, show my boyfriend what I'd been looking at, and have us watch it together while we had sex, but I think he'd freak out if he saw I was into German gang bangs," said one girl.

I have a feeling she's right. One time my boyfriend came over and went to use my computer while I was cooking us dinner. It needed to be plugged in and charged because it had died the night before, and when it finally came to life, I suddenly heard loud moanings coming out of it. I quickly looked up. "Oh, crap," I thought. I'd forgotten it had died when I was drunkenly cruising XTube the night before.

"Um, excuse me?" my boyfriend said, slowly turning the computer to face me. I cringed. What the hell had I been looking at? I breathed a great sigh of relief when it turned out to be straight and normal, just a girl giving a guy a blow. Phew.

"Oh yeah, I must have been looking at that before I fell asleep last night. Does that bother you?" I asked, chopping away at our dinner nonchalantly, even though I was red in the face at being blatantly caught looking at porn.

"No, of course not," he said grinning. Oh, brother.

Women are supposed to hate pornography, and most men assume that we all find it degrading and offensive. If only they knew how much Dirty Girls are freely checking out online smut—some of it truly hardcore—then we might all be able to incorporate it into our sex lives a bit and feel less creepy about what we enjoy looking at.

The Weirdest Places Women Have Done It

I once wrote an article for *Details* about men who choke the chicken at work. I found many men who admitted that sometimes when they were bored or had been perusing a naughty site, they went to the handicapped stall at work and rubbed one out (while pretending to just be taking a dump). The truth was, I wasn't surprised. Work can be boring. Once, way back when I was waiting tables at the age of eighteen, things were so slow, and I was so bored that I snuck into the bathroom and went for it myself. I asked other women if they'd done something like that at work, and if not, where the weirdest places they'd masturbated were. I found out that a ton of them really did it whenever the mood struck, regardless of where they were, which seems an awful lot like what men might do. Of course, they did do their best to keep themselves totally hidden. Women, unlike some twisted men, do not get off from exposing themselves in public and masturbating on the subway. Here are some of the places they did do it:

"I once did it at work. I was dirty messaging with this guy and I had a private cube. It was just hands over the pants action, but it worked."

"On an airplane. The seats kicked back, it was a serious long flight, and I had the blanket to cover my actions. Most people were sleeping."

"In the car in a parking lot. I'd just bought a new vibrator at the mall and wanted to test it out."

"Backseat of the car on a road trip. My parents were driving and my little brother was sleeping next to me. I was reading a racy novel."

"In the sauna when a bunch of people were playing pool right outside the door."

"Stationary bike at the gym."

"Shower at the gym."

"Steam room at the gym."

"In an auditorium class in college. Boring lecture."

HAVE YOUR MAN READ THIS, PLEASE: WOMEN, MASTURBATION, AND PORN

So, now you know one of our dirtiest secrets: women often masturbate like bonobo monkeys, and a lot of the time, we do it while we're reading filthy material or looking at porn on the computer. Some women even have secret files of videos hidden away in our hard drives—like my friend who took her laptop into work to see if the IT guys could fix something, and they pointed out that her collection of anal porn had give her computer a virus.

This is nothing to be upset about, and even better, it could totally be something the two of you can use to help spice up your sex life. Just remember that when women look at porn, it's pretty much always strictly fantasy. In reality, we don't really want anything or anyone sleazy near our respectable selves. We are not secretly meeting three men in hotel rooms during the workday for a quickie gang bang, and we're not going down to Chinatown for a cheap happy ending. We're also not using Craigslist Casual Encounters to meet random partners. Allow me to reiterate: it's fantasy.

And that's why, even if you discover that her favorite thing is to look at anal porn, you're really still not getting anywhere near her butt. And those threesomes might turn you both on, but the chances of her ever actually going through with one are about slim to none. Go ahead and enjoy looking at pics or videos together, just don't ever pressure her into doing the things you are watching unless you want her to break down and cry. And never make comparisons to the women you see in them and say something like, "Why can't you take it in the bunghole like she does?" because the answer is, "Why don't you have a twelve-inch wiener and shave your balls like he does?" Do you really want to go there?

Chapter Seven

Picking Up Dirty Girls

We Are Far More Complicated
Than Men Think

For one of my *Maxim* articles, I wrote about how guys need to step up their game when it comes to picking up women, and by that, I did not mean following the rules of *The Game*, which is the pick-up artist's handbook and basically teaches men of all ages how to be complete and utter douche bags. While I was doing my research on the art of picking up chicks, I was surprised to find out how much bad advice was out there when it comes to hitting on the ladies. So I interviewed a bunch of Dirty Girls to find out what really worked on them and what it was that made a guy appealing enough to sleep with—or date, whatever.

First of all, the most important thing I found was

that people need to realize that picking up someone is not as simple as having a sense of humor, which is what all men's and women's magazines—and online articles on how to get laid or find love—would like you to believe. If that were the case, then Carrot Top would have no shortage of admirers and lovers. Yes, having a sense of humor is a lovely thing, and something that everyone in the world likes in their partners. What woman would honestly say that she wants to be with a humorless stick-up-the-ass mate?

But none of these articles touched on other equally important things that women hold dear when looking for a mate, such as what his face looks like, whether he is fit or obese, short or long and lanky. And quite important is whether he is sporting a micropenis or is of average size. The truth is, women can be just as shallow as men when it comes to looks, body type, and dick size. And all of this matters when guys are trying to pick us up. OK, so he doesn't have to be a male model (trust me—I once went on a date with a model who was so dumb I could barely get through one drink with him), but it helps if he is normal looking, wears normal clothes, has a normal job (or just a job, really), and has a normal penis. But to be honest, it really helps if he is hot, stylish, has a cool job, or is packing a gigantic pistol.

Where Men Got It Wrong: What Not to Do to Impress a Woman

I found out that there are an awful lot of younger guys out there who, thanks to the Internet and idiotic MTV shows like *The Pick Up Artist*, have decided that pick-up artistry is awesome and will help them get laid. They follow the guru Mystery, who wears fuzzy Dr. Seuss hats and black eyeliner and lots of jelly bracelets. Reality check: most women actually find Dr. Seuss hats to be the biggest turnoff in the world. Also, men should not attempt to use the "neg," a shitty insult in disguise, as a means of getting a woman interested in them.

Apparently the neg is supposed to appeal to a woman's insecurities. This show convinced oodles of men that such tactics actually worked, and young and impressionable guys will believe anything and do anything to stick their penis into someone. The following list shows some popular negs that I found online:

1. *Your hair looks shiny. Is it a wig? Oh, well, it looks nice anyway.*

   See how this is supposed to be an insult but then quickly turns into a compliment? Classic neg. Who the hell wears a wig? The response to this is laughing out loud at the pure absurdity of it. Maybe say, "No, but I am wearing a pubic wig."

2. *You have U-shaped teeth.*

   Sorry, what? Seriously, this one doesn't make sense to me. What are U-shaped teeth? I think a Trekkie nerd wrote this one. I don't even have a witty response as I imagine no man will ever say this to you. If he does, walk away because he scares me.

3. *You have an interesting figure.*

   A guy once told me I had a swimmer's body. When I asked what that meant, he said I had broad shoulders and looked buff. He was hitting on me, and he thought that by telling me I looked buff I'd be smitten. I wasn't. At least he wasn't calling me Large Marge, but why mention my body at all unless he's telling me I have the nicest ass he's ever seen? No woman wants to be told she has broad shoulders. It makes her feel like a linebacker. Needless to say, I did not have sex with him.

4. *I think I like your left eye best.*

This one's an insult to me—I have a weird twitch in my right eye that makes it kind of squish up and go all squinty when I smile, and I usually hope most people don't notice. But this neg doesn't make sense. It's like telling a guy, "I like your left nut best." Who has a preference?

5. *Were you a dork in school?*

The guy here is trying to tease the girl and make her feel embarrassed or like a dork, and then he is supposed to hit on her and make her feel special. This is a really lame line, and the proper answer should be, "Yes, is it that easy to recognize a fellow loser?"

6. *You remind me of my weird ex.*

This. Line. Does. Not. Work. On. Anyone. Ever.

7. *You look like my high school math teacher.*

If his resembled mine, this would mean you look like a tiny, poodle-haired fifty-year-old woman named Mrs. Lloyd who pointed only with her middle finger. The proper response is "Wow, she must have been fucking hot. How did you concentrate on fractions?"

8. *How short are you, anyway?*

   A woman's stature should never be questioned. The proper response: "I'm about eye to eye with your man tits. How short are you?"

9. *Those shoes look really comfortable.*

   This is actually a terrific insult from one woman to another—snide, totally bitchy, yet under the guise of complimentary. But from a man, any comment on your clothes (other than "That's an awesome dress" or "Your legs look fantastic in that skirt") is simply weird. Anyway, proper response: "They actually are. I have inverted arches. It's very painful, and these help a lot."

10. *I like your shirt. Is it from H&M?*

    What can I say, I'm a sucker for both the fashionable and the affordable, and this wouldn't insult me in the least. However, some guys think they are insulting you by asking if you are wearing cheap clothing. They are sending the message that they are into designer clothes. Proper response: "Are your slacks L.L.Bean?"

What I actually found when interviewing women is that the only tactic women actually respond to when guys are picking them up are *compliments*. It's like bacon—we can't help but love it. Even when a construction guy walks by us and tells us we're beautiful—hell, even if he says, "Hey baby, nice ass," Dirty Girls derive serious pleasure from it. A guy can ask me if I have synthetic hair or if I'm faster than Michael Phelps all he likes—he's not getting in my pants. But tell me that I'm hot, and chances are he's at least getting some French kissing out of it.

"I know they do it to every woman who walks by, but I can't help but smile when someone passes me on the street and whistles or says something about my body," says a good friend of mine. "I don't find it insulting or negative in the least. Bring it on!" Almost everyone I talk to agreed. We don't care who says it or what they even say. Catcalling usually makes us feel good about ourselves—as long as we are not alone in a dark alley with a gang of rapidly approaching men. After all, they are basically compliments!

We Are Shallow: Clothes Do Make the Man

We like men who know how to dress well. For most of us, this doesn't mean he has to rock Armani suits or Prada leather jackets—Dirty Girls are often lucky to even have something that is both cool and clean to wear themselves on any given night—but a guy must know how to pull off a pair of jeans, have some shoes that aren't white sneakers, and not tuck his T-shirts into his drawstring pants. If a guy we're interested in does dress like a tool, we're not going to automatically write him off—well, most of us aren't. One friend dumped a guy over his square-toed Aldo boots. But we will make slight adjustments to his wardrobe, either by buying him cool shirts we like or by sometimes just throwing out something we think is gross. I did this once to a guy who had a Charlie Brown T-shirt, with the same zigzag pattern and colors. Because his head was slightly round, when he wore it he seriously resembled a Peanuts character. And so one morning, I stuffed it in the bottom of the garbage can. Was that immature? Shallow? I don't care. All I know for sure is that, good grief, no one wants to fuck Charlie Brown. And I never had to again.

Those guys who tend to follow the pick-up artist handbooks and dish out negs also like to do something their guru calls peacocking, or dressing for attention. According to the rules, sometimes this means wearing a piece of flair, like a unique "badge" that might pique a woman's interest. Such guys really hope you might approach them and say, "Oh look, a badge! Now what does that cool badge mean?" The peacock might then reply, "Well, funny you should ask about my badge. My four-year-old niece gave it to me. It's a good luck charm that's supposed to protect me from fast cars and fast women." "Tee hee!" a woman will supposedly reply. "Fast women like me you mean?" "Yes," the pick-up artist responds. "Now let's go back to my place and screw." "OK!" she will cry, just because he wore a badge!

I don't know about you, but the only fellow with a badge who I'll give the time of day to is a cop who's giving me a speeding ticket. What might peacocking guys wear? I looked up "peacocking outfits" online and found items like a snap-on studded belt with grommets and a yin-yang pendant. These are things a girl might have worn proudly with her shoe boots in the 1990s, straight out of Contempo Casuals. None of these things are sexy or stylish. If a guy is serious about getting a girl's attention, he needs to leave the fuzzy top hats to the stoners playing with their devil sticks and just wear something normal, like jeans and a T-shirt or a button-down. It's not that hard!

When Men Flirt with Our Friends We Get Annoyed

A lot of men think that flirting with a woman's friends is a clever pick-up maneuver: they hit on her friend or friends. The handbook calls this active disinterest, which sometimes includes a man downright ignoring the woman he's actually interested in and other times involves certain sleazy moves like making hard eye contact with a girl, gazing at her lips, and then smiling and quickly turning away to convey the message "not gonna happen." Then the guy flirts with her friends, and the target is supposed to get jealous because she knows she's made some sort of connection and will try her best to cut in and get the pick-up artist's attention.

Phew—this is a really complicated way to get an insecure and needy chick interested in you. According to all the women I know, if a cute guy spent most of his time ignoring them and talking to their friends, they would assume disinterest and move along. If he then tried to come on to her too, they'd be confused or think he was a jerk. Dirty Girls may be down for a lot of things, but screwing over their friends for a one-night stand isn't usually in the cards. However, if a woman is genuinely interested in the same guy her friend is, and he likes her back, then she will usually go for it—hopefully after conferring with her pal. As long as there is real interest on one woman's part, it is fair game to ask someone to step aside. After all, hos before bros.

A Cautionary Tale about Hos before Bros

There have been two times in my life that I admit I truly did not follow the adage hos before bros. One was a summer fling I barely remember—he was the very recent ex of a girl I had just become friendly with, and I was about to go back to school when he and I got drunk and hooked up. To make up for it, I introduced her to a charming friend of mine, and she got laid herself. No harm done—in fact she thanked me for sleeping with her ex because she had a huge crush on the guy I set her up with and wanted to make sure the ex was totally out of the way and wouldn't be hurt that she was moving on so fast.

The other was during summer break of high school. The ultimate high school hottie was home for the summer, and my girlfriend and I went to his house to smoke pot. She had been in love with him for about three years, so really I was just there for moral support so she could flirt with him and I could get stoned. Well, we all ended up watching a movie and passing out, the guy in the middle of us girls. When I awoke, he was squished up close to me, and I don't know if it was the pot or the summer heat but I suddenly really wanted to make out with him. My friend had to leave to go home and as she got up, she asked if I was coming with her. I said I was too tired still, and after she glared at me and stormed out of there, he and I kissed for the next half hour or so.

Later when she grilled me about what had happened, I lied and told her I'd just kept napping and went home half an hour later. She could tell I was lying and I felt awful, and it was nearly a year before we became tight again.

For the most part, hos before bros (or chicks before dicks) is something I firmly believe in. Yes, I wanted a piece of the high school hottie, and I lied to my friend to get a little. Still, it's not something I would do again, no matter how clouded my judgment was from toking a big spliff. And for the record, like a lot of high school hotties, this one ended up prematurely bald and unattractive, and my friend and I are still together.

Talk about Sex

In college, I once took a guy friend of mine home because he was straight-up honest about sex, about how good it would be between us and how his favorite thing to do was go down on a girl. Also, he told me his dick was the size of a baby's arm, and let's be honest, the idea of that totally turned me on. I excitedly took him home for a promising night of sex. We started making out, and I kind of felt down there. "Huh?" I thought. "Baby's arm?" It was more like a baby's dick. The guy had lied to me straight up, and I'd foolishly fallen for it. I made up some excuse for him to leave, and we never got past a little light French kissing. I would say that's the last time a guy bamboozled me into hooking up with him because he promised yummy sex, but I'd be lying.

Many men's magazine stories say things like, "Women hate to be objectified! Don't make them feel like sex objects! If the first thing out of your mouth is something sexually related, she's going to be so turned off and think you're a jerk. Women like nice guys! Sex, ew!"

Please. I know many Dirty Girls who have hooked up with a guy simply because he said something that turned them on so much they decided to go ahead and let them see, touch, or feel their lady parts right then and there. Some lines are just what we're looking for. "You look like you'd be so fucking good in bed" has worked on my friends more than once. And then there was "I'd give a million dollars just to see what kind of panties you're wearing." After thinking for a second and determining they weren't my standby cotton panties that come in packs of five from Wal-Mart, I gave him a little peek outside of my waistband. "Mmm," he groaned. "Those are so hot." We never hooked up, and he was cute enough that I probably would have—if only to show him I was also wearing a matching bra.

"My favorite line ever was by this guy who came up to me at a party and just said, 'This place sucks. Let's go somewhere where we can fuck,'" says Sarah, a thirty-year-old friend of mine. "We totally grabbed hands and left the party and hopped into a cab and went back to his place and did just that." A guy once approached another friend saying, "Your ass in that skirt has to be the hottest thing I have seen in a long time." "He was hot, I was buzzed, and it turned me on to think I was turning him on so much," she says. "I love flattery and I don't care if it comes in some sort of 'sexist' package. If a guy thinks I'm hot and wants to tell me so, it's somewhat likely that I will reward his compliments in some kind of physical way. If I'm attracted to him, of course. Unfortunately, those lines don't work for the ugly turds in the room."

Even when it's about sex, it all comes back to compliments. Compliments are just the best way to a gal's heart and loins. Flattery is one of those universally liked things that simply never gets old. Being told we're beautiful, have nice bodies, or are sexy appeals to our most basic instinct: ego! If a guy strokes that properly, it's possible we'll be stroking something of his in return.

Women and One-Night Stands

Most men would be surprised to find out how many Dirty Girls are interested in having sex with them one time, just to see if it was any good, and then never dealing with them again. Women are supposed to think that one-nighters are dirty and should make us feel used and bad about ourselves, but I know plenty of women who actually love to hook up with guys when the mood strikes them and then not have to deal with them the morning after. I wrote a well-received *Maxim* article on this once. Basically, the gist of it was that woman have one-night stands fairly often. Sometimes we like them and brag about them the next day. Sometimes they are utter disasters and we totally cry afterward. But they happen, and they happen often.

The Best One-Night Stand Ever

My best one-night stand ever was years ago, when I was at Burning Man—the crazy nonstop party held for a week each year out in the Nevada desert (shut up—I was nineteen). I don't even recall how I met Wills because I think I was on mushrooms at the time, and it was Burning Man, so who knows how these things happen, but he happened to be staying in an awesome Winnebago while I was staying in some cold and dusty cramped tent. So after hanging out with him and his friends for a while, I was more than happy to go back to his well-sheltered bed. The night was mainly memorable because he was good in the sack, and there was that whole bed instead of a sleeping bag appeal. He was super tender and into everything, and it was all light and fun and funny. (Again—I was on mushrooms, but still.)

The next morning, I woke up to fresh-squeezed orange juice, coffee, and a toasted bagel with cream cheese. He was also wearing a sarong, so that was a demerit, but I just chalked it up to his being a Euro, and kind of a hippie at Burning Man, I guess. I enjoyed my breakfast in the warm sun, and sat with him for a while before I told him I had to leave and find my friends, wherever they were. He gave me a kiss on the cheek and told me he'd had a great time, and that I knew where to find him if I wanted to come back later that night. I smiled and shrugged. I said I might be back, feeling happy and powerful that the decision had been left to me, and that he wasn't trying to make it anything it wasn't. I knew only his first name, and that he was from England and looked like Sting. We'd had good sex. That was enough. That is what an awesome one-night-stand is supposed to be like. Curling up in a ball and crying over how your one-nighters never want anything more from you than to hook up is not the goal.

Of course, it's easier when you're on vacation or in a place like Burning Man where the chance of bumping into your one-night amour on the subway or at a local restaurant is less likely. Ego can also get in the way of making one-night stands a success. Even if a woman doesn't want to see or sleep with a guy again, knowing that the guy doesn't want to see or sleep with her again is annoying.

The Serial One-Night-Stand Girl

Some people don't have a problem with serial one-night stands. Case in point: my very close friend who likes to bring guys back to her place all the time for a quick roll in the hay after closing time. For her, it's just about having a nice orgasm before she falls asleep.

"It's easy to find someone willing to come back to my place when the bar is closing down," my girlfriend says about picking up her flings. "There are always stragglers who are interested in having one more drink, or sometimes I ask if they want to get a slice of pizza across the street from my place," she says. "Then I'll ask them up for a nightcap. Sometimes I don't even get their names, and we just go up to my place and start going for it. Sometimes they stay the night and leave in the morning, which is what I like best. I don't like when a guy sneaks out in the middle of the night, even though I've picked them up for sex. There are still etiquette rules!"

She also hates it when a guy hangs around the next day for too long, expecting to go to brunch and then shopping and then maybe dinner and then to start calling her sweetie by the day's end. "I had that happen to me once, and the problem was I really liked the guy I hooked up with. So I stuck around and we had brunch, and then I went shopping with him for curtains. While we were out, he bought a toothbrush for me and said something about not having to use his the next time I was over. I was getting pretty excited about where the whole thing was going already, and then I never really heard from him again. That went horribly wrong," she said.

My best friend, Marie, used to have regular one-night stands too, and she was always disappointed by the size of the guy she brought home. But she had really high big-dick standards.

"Why can't guys just wear a sign on their sleeve that says 'packing' or 'small peen?'" she asked me once.

"Because that's like us having to wear signs that say 'super dangly labia,'" I told her. "Guys are sensitive about that. Plus, not *all* tiny willies are terrible," I said.

"Who do you think you're talking to, a man? Yes they are," she said. "I just can't stand it when I get a guy home and he has a teeny one. And you honestly can't tell from their stature or the size of their hands or even their attitudes. Like that guy Richard, remember the super short dude?"

I did indeed. He wore socks in bed with her.

"Yes, wee Richard," I said. "What about him?"

"Well, he was short, but since you never know, I gave it a try and was totally pleasantly surprised by the size of his thing. It was above average, and he knew what he was doing with it too," she said.

"So why did you never answer his calls again?" I asked.

"When I looked at his Hanes T-shirt on the floor, I saw that it was a boy's size," she said. "He shopped in the boys' department. And that's why."

Marie also once had a problem with a one-nighter that wouldn't leave, and because I was living with her at the time, it soon became my problem just as much as it was hers. She'd met a guy through mutual friends at a party and brought him back to our place. The next day was Saturday, and I was lounging around on the couch watching TV, eating toast, and being generally lazy. Marie's door was ajar, but I didn't think anything about openly farting while I was lying there. I eventually got up to shower, and when I came out, wrapped in a towel, I started to make coffee when I heard someone come out of her room.

"Oh, hey," I said, not looking behind me.

"Um, hi," came a deep voice that caused me to swing around and screech. There stood a burly dude in a wrinkly set of clothes.

"I'm James," he said. "Marie's friend."

"Oh," I said. "Where's Marie?"

"She had to go out somewhere and told me I could sleep in," he said.

Well, I guess that was fine, I thought. Not a huge deal. He'd be leaving now that he was awake.

"Oh, cool, well nice to meet you. I have to get dressed and go to brunch, so see you later," I said, backing into my bedroom. But when I got dressed and came out, the guy was still there, watching TV.

"OK, well, I have to go now, so…" I waited for him to get up and leave with me.

"OK, bye," he said. "Marie said she'd be back soon, so maybe I'll see you later."

What the fuck was wrong with this guy? I furiously texted Marie on the way to brunch.

"Sorry, he's just visiting from New York. Guess he has no place to stay," she said.

Great. The out-of-towner one-night stand. Talk about the guy who overstays his welcome.

The One-Night Stand Who Doesn't Leave

Most of the time when Dirty Girls have one-night stands, we expect them to be just that. One night of doing it with a stranger (sometimes a friend!), and then the guy leaves when the two of you wake up in the morning. But occasionally a guy will decide, for whatever reason, to just hang around for the rest of the day, which makes things really awkward.

A friend recently told me, "You have no idea how awful it was. It was Saturday morning, so I didn't have the work excuse to get rid of him. At first it was kind of sweet—he wanted to cuddle. So I let him spoon me, but after fifteen minutes of that, I started to feel awkward about it, so I got up to make some coffee. He then proceeded to get on my couch and put my blanket over him, grab the remote, and settle in for a little casual tube time. So I told him I had to shower, thinking he would be dressed by the time I was out. But no. He was watching football! I gently told him I had no idea what football was about and that I never watched it, hoping he'd get the hint and watch it somewhere else. Instead, he proceeded to explain the rules of football. Has anyone tried to explain the rules of football to you? It's all yards and mathematical shit. So finally I said, 'Look, I really had fun, but I need to do some errands and have to take my laundry down.' So he walked down with me, and I thought he was finally bailing when he walked right into the Laundromat and started to sort through my nasty dirty undies and tell me that I should really use Tide stick on stains! My period stains!" That's when she lost it. She told him she was sorry but she really had to have some alone time. He finally got the hint. She then said, "He called to tell me he got home OK. Then he called three times a day for two weeks in a row and finally left me a text that just said, 'Fuck you, bitch.' Dudes are crazy."

Erectile Dysfunction (and Other Awkward Moments with One-Night Stands)

I hate to say it, but for a woman, there is really nothing worse than bringing a guy back to her place for a quickie and him not being able to get it up.

These things are supposed to be hot, throwdown, tussle kinds of events, not awkward moments where we sit there naked and watch a man try and rub himself to a proper degree of hardness so we can do it. That's not to say it's totally abnormal—a lot of times when a woman meets a guy out, and they both decide to go home and have sex, generally there has been a lot of drinking going on. And nothing takes the sail out of a man's ween like whiskey and Coke. But, man, are those moments depressing for a woman.

"I had a weekend fling with a guy who hardly got hard at all, even though we kept trying," says a girlfriend of mine. "The worst part was that he kept saying, 'This never happens to me,' and so I sadly assumed it was my fault and that he wasn't attracted to *me*." No matter what the excuse is—whiskey-Coke dick, antidepressants, performance anxiety—women will always think that it is their fault to a degree, that the guy is just simply not that into her, which totally deflates the ego.

"I hate when a guy is limp during a one-night stand!" my friend Kathy agreed. "Why the hell does he think I brought him home? Certainly not to make small talk and hear excuses for his ED."

HAVE YOUR MALE FRIENDS READ THIS, PLEASE: TIPS ON PICKING UP WOMEN

For those of you with guy friends who could step up their game a little bit, here is a handy cheat sheet on what not to do to get a girl to go home with you, either for a one-night stand or for the beginning of a beautiful relationship.

1   Do not have a limp dick.
2. Do not wear stupid pieces of clothing like large hats, chokers, or badges.
3   Do not insult her or attempt to give her a neg. Compliments only.
4. Do not have a limp dick.
5. Do not stay for the entire weekend if she agrees to bring you home.

And just because I know you could use some actual advice, here are things to do to get a woman into bed.

1. Compliment her in a believable way. If things are flirty, you can bring up sex—say something about how much she turns you on or how good she smells. We know

you're thinking about getting naked with us, or at least we're hoping you are if we are flirting back.

2. Keep your eyes on her all night. She'll eventually glance over at you, and then if she keeps glancing back, she's down to talk and make out.

3. Buy her a drink—easy, charming, and cheap.

4. Wear something normal. It's better that she perceives you as a somewhat safe dresser than one who still shops at Hot Topic.

5. If possible, let it slip that you have a big penis, but don't lie about it.

Chapter Eight

What Women Want in Bed

Put Down the *Kama Sutra* Because
There's No Way We're Doing the
Wheelbarrow with You Tonight

*L*et's talk about sex. Yes, some more. Sex is an interesting subject for women. We're told through studies that men think about sex 250 times a day and that women think about it 6 times a day—always with her partner in the missionary position, and then she reads the Bible because she feels so guilty about it. I have been a sex columnist for two years, and I have interviewed many women about their sexual habits. I can say one thing with certainty—six times a day is simply not true. Some Dirty Girls think about sex all the time, sometimes from the time they wake up until the time they go to bed. Granted, a lot of times they might be thinking about how they can get out of having to do it that night, but regardless, they're thinking about it! This chapter explores all sorts of aspects about women and sex: how much they want it, how they want it, who they want it with, and how often they're actually doing it.

How Much They Want It

You know what I hate? Married male comedians. They always talk about the same thing—how their wives don't want to have sex with them anymore. "'Not tonight dear, I have a headache.' You have a headache, what about my ball ache!'" they always seem to say, in a horrible whiny voice to imitate their wives. I always watch these dudes, who tend to be gingers with wispy hair, and think, "No, guy, she probably just doesn't want to have sex with you anymore." Women enjoy sex, and as far as I know, they are into having it on a regular basis.

But that doesn't mean we don't get bored by it with the same person night after night. And nothing is worse than when our boyfriends or husbands seem to lose interest in doing it with us as much as they used to. When that happens, generally around the three-and-a-half-year mark, we initially feel slighted and unattractive and wonder why they don't want to do it with us anymore. Then we get suspicious and wonder where they are getting it, because they once wanted a beej every night, and now they lazily roll over for a hump in the dark about once a week. We suspect that they are spending far too much time spanking to porn or have someone or something on the side. But the worst part is, we're still horny. And when they don't seem to want to give it to us, well, it's just depressing. We don't want to have to always initiate. We want them to want us as much as we want them. And the less active they are, the less active it makes us, and then it becomes a major issue and people cheat or break up. It's truly a vicious cycle!

I was talking to a friend about this, and she agreed that she always seemed to want it more than her boyfriend—until the day she decided she wasn't in love with him anymore. Then she couldn't bring herself to touch him. And unfortunately, because she didn't get the balls to break up with him until a long time after that, she spent nearly a year and a half avoiding sex with him at all costs.

"You should have seen me try to cock block him on Valentine's Day," she told me. "Do you know how hard that is? It's an entire holiday devoted to having sex. Yes, there are flowers and candy and dinners, but it all boils down to being forced by society to hump. They say it's a Hallmark holiday but it has become a *Penthouse* holiday."

"How did you manage to get out of it that night?" I asked.

"It was hard. I basically plied him with wine. I ordered another bottle when we were close to leaving, and then I ordered dessert. Then I made him stop off for nightcaps with me and insisted we do shots. I got him so drunk that by the time we got home he just blacked out. It was a success, but the whole night I was just fraught, thinking, 'Oh, God, he's so going to want to do it when we get home.'"

But most of my girlfriends in long relationships actually say they want it more than their lazy mates do these days.

How Often Do We Want It?

"It depends on how long I've been in the relationship to be honest," said Amanda, a thirty-year-old friend who has had a few long-term relationships. "At the beginning of my last relationship, we were doing it every night. Sometimes twice a day on the weekends," she tells me. "That lasted for about a year. Then it tapered off, and by the third year of the relationship, we were down to about twice a week. Sometimes once a week. Sometimes less. The sad thing was, I was usually the one who wanted it more than he did."

I understood. I'd had some experiences where I wanted to get laid and was shot down cold turkey by an old boyfriend. The worst was when, one time after an argument, I tried to go in for the usually awesome makeup sex. We'd made up earlier, and he was reading a book when I came into the bedroom in a black lacy matching bra and panty set. I slunk over to where he was and started kissing him, feeling super sexy and ready for my makeup action. He just grunted and rolled over.

"What's the matter?" I asked, kissing his neck.

"I'm not in the mood," he huffed. "I'm still upset from our argument earlier!"

I have to say, I was quite taken aback. He was pulling what seemed like a seriously girl move when I was dressed up as a fantasy chick. I offered to just go down, you know, just to get him out of his pissy huff.

"No. I just want to read and go to sleep," he pouted.

Fuck that! That is not the way any woman wants to be treated when it comes to sex. We feel that if we want it, we should be able to get it. It's the woman's job to turn the men down, at least that's what we're raised to believe. The problem is, I don't know many women who will turn it down when offered. But I'm starting to know a lot more men who will. Why is this? I decided to check in with some of my guy friends to see what happened to their libidos when they were in a relationship.

"You won't believe it but something seemed to happen when I turned thirty-four," said my friend Matt, a serial dater whose last relationship had gone severely south and left him brokenhearted. "My dick just wasn't as eager anymore, and I have no idea why," he said. "I'm chalking it up to age, which is sad, because I never thought I'd be that kind of person who got too old to want to screw. I always prided myself on being super horny and up for anything at any time. It's not like I suffer from erectile dysfunction; I just am not as horny as I used to be. Well, sometimes I guess I do get ED."

"Oh. Ew. Sorry. I know that happens. That sucks," I said.

"Yeah, it happens sometimes. It really sucks; you

have no idea. There's no way to convince a girl that you're really attracted to her and want to have sex when your dick is laying there like a dead worm."

With that rather unattractive vision in mind, I left the conversation and returned to my friends to ask what they did when they found themselves face-to-face with a dead worm.

Women and the Dreaded ED

I recently sent a text to a friend of mine who had just started seeing this guy and was spending her first weekend away with him upstate: "How's everything going?"

A few minutes later her reply buzzed in: "He's amazing. But sex is awful."

Oh no. She really liked him, and all of our friends were hoping that this one might actually work out, because she hadn't had a boyfriend in more than a year, and we were a little nervous that she was becoming bitter and turning off potential suitors.

"Crap. Well, sex always gets better," I said reassuringly, or hopefully reassuringly. She wrote back almost immediately: "He has anxiety issues and can't get it up."

Oh, dear. I didn't know what to say to that.

When she returned, we went out and talked about it all more in depth. She explained that everything else about their weekend had been amazing, that he was one of the smartest and nicest people she'd ever known, and that they got along so well. But he had serious problems in the bedroom. She tried talking to him about it, but it just made things more awkward.

"So how did you leave it?" I asked.

"We broke up," she said.

"Oh no!" I cried. "I really thought you guys were going to make it."

"Yeah, well, it turned out there was just too much emotional neediness on his part. I'm not cut out for that. If you can't get hard for me, I really can't get hard for you either," she said.

The Truth about Foreplay

Foreplay, foreplay, foreplay. Most men are probably so sick of reading about the damn ten-minute session where they need to be selfless and devote some attention to their ladies, when they are horny now and want to stick it in, damn it. Plus, it starts to sound kind of hokey and new agey. "Don't forget the foreplay!" cries out basically every single article in every single men's magazine on how to pleasure a woman. But you know why it's written about so bloody often? Because it works. Maybe we need a sexier term for it than foreplay, which sounds like some kind of golf lingo. Let's call it preheating.

Preheating doesn't need to be boring, it doesn't need to be a pain in the ass, and it's not necessary to devote lots of attention and time to it every single time. If a woman isn't in the mood for preheating and wants to just go right into the deep boning, she'll go ahead and let the guy know that, most likely by sitting on his penis. But the majority of women love a little preheating sexual action, and it comes in many forms, none of which is designed to be annoying for the man (read: preheating doesn't just mean giving her oral).

I asked a bunch of women what their men did to totally turn them on before they got it on. "Touch my boobs," said Sally. "All a guy needs to do is run his hand over my sweater and I'm already starting to get wet in anticipation. If he goes under my shirt and bra and gently pinches and rubs my nipples, I get gooey, and if he licks them, I'm screwed. Or I'm about to be."

The breasts are the most sensitive erogenous

zone outside of the clitoris, and given any kind of attention, they will loosen up the rest of our bodies for limber and enthusiastic sex. A man just has to treat them as if they were special and recognize that they are as sensitive as they are, which means touch them in a gentle but firm manner.

Most Dirty Girls like the breast attention, but other women tend to also like some sort of attention down below the belt. To all men, this means immediately pulling down her underwear and sticking one or two fingers up inside her. This is not what I mean. This starts to feel good only once we've already been properly turned on and are wet and looking for something to fill us up. If it comes at us too soon, it not only doesn't feel great but also just feels bad. And it makes the guy seem like an amateur.

"I like it when a guy sort of plays with the waistband of my panties without actually shoving his hands down there too quickly," said Jane, a girl I know who I wouldn't describe as chaste. She likes sex, and she has it often, whether or not she has a boyfriend. "I can't stand it when a guy thinks the best way to get me wet is to just shove a finger inside me. If I want something up inside me, then why wouldn't I prefer a nice dick to a skinny pointer finger?"

Many men are great with their hands and fingers and can bring women to orgasm that way, but it's not easy. The area needs to be lubed (which is why oral is so awesome—it's lubricating and stimulating at once), and truth be told, a lot of women are germaphobes who can't get turned on thinking of fingers up inside them when they know those same fingers were just putting together beef patties for dinner. Whispering, "Wash your hands first, baby," is the least sexual thing we could ever say in the heat of the moment, so sometimes we'll just let you go ahead and do it even though it makes us squeamish, and we are nervous about cooties.

When a guy is down there during preheating, he should never take a cue from his favorite girl-on-girl porn and smack her vaginal area. I don't know why they do this in porn movies. I've never met a single girl who thought this was a sexy, stimulating move. It simply isn't.

Another thing women told me they hated in the sack was any kind of dry rub. Lube is obviously the best option, and most of us keep some on hand, but that takes away the possibility of getting oral somewhere in the sexual encounter. We all know that shit tastes nasty and wouldn't subject our poor dudes to poisonous-tasting lube. This is why I'm hesitant to break out the lube ever, unless I am positive there is zero chance of the guy going down. However, I don't mind the spit. I know it sounds gross, but it's free, it's plentiful, and it's right there. The only real problem with spit is that, when it starts to dry up, it often starts to smell like a shoe with dog poo on it. So, he has to keep the spit going to keep the area moist or use a woman's natural lube to keep things wet. Nothing is grosser that being horny, preheating, and catching a whiff of poo.

One girl told me she loved dry humping as a form of preheating. I hadn't used that term since high school! But I knew what she meant. Pressing crotches together and being able to feel his manhood through his pants is seriously sexy, no matter how old you are.

"If I'm making out with a guy, I can sit on top of him, clothes on, and rub up against his crotch, and I have to stop myself from coming that way," she said. "The entire combo of French kissing, him kissing my neck, his hands on my breasts, and the feel of his boner pressing into me—I swear that sometimes I think it's actually better than sex. Because when we eventually start having sex he's so wrapped up in just sliding in and out of me that he forgets to kiss me, he completely ignores my tits, and I don't really have anything putting pressure on my clit. So yeah, sometimes I prefer to dry hump over real hump."

Sexual Positions

Ask a lot of women what their favorite sexual position is, and you'll get no general consensus that one way is better than the other. Many women love one position for a certain reason, and others love another for a completely different reason. However, all of the women I've talked to agree that they aren't into weird and newfangled maneuvers that seem uncomfortable or allow for extra-deep stimulation. So tell your men to throw away that stupid *Kama Sutra*—there's not a very good chance that she'll get down on her forearms for a little reverse cowgirl tonight.

Women on Top

Women love to be on top in life, so why wouldn't we enjoy it in bed? A good 30 percent of the women I polled on their favorite sexual positions said they loved to be on top, just because it's the best way to really feel in control of where the pressure from the guy's lower body area hits their clitoris. They also think the guy likes the view of them bouncing around on top of them, and seeing their guy's horny faces from that angle gets them worked up too.

"I love being on top because my boyfriend always looks at me and tells me I look hot," said a friend of mine. She said it's probably because she always plays with her own breasts when she's up there, and that gets him all turned on.

"I like it because I can also position myself to touch myself at the same time," said another girl I know. "I can't really get off from anything other than having direct clit stimulation, either through touching myself or having him go down on me, so this way, I can actually enjoy the feeling of penetration while I'm basically masturbating. Plus, he thinks it's hot when I do that at the same time. Win-win."

Not so for another friend of mine, who said she regularly touched herself or used a vibrator while she was on top with her ex-boyfriend. "I thought it was super hot and that he'd think I was a sex goddess and all that, but it turned out it just pissed him off, because he thought that I should be able to come just from riding up and down his boner," she says. "He once asked me, 'Do we really need that again?' when I whipped out my favorite finger vibe while I was on top. I told him yes, actually. It didn't do much to save our already failing relationship."

My friend who used to hump her teddy bear said the reason she liked women on top so much was that it was just like those good old days with Rufus—she could smoosh her pelvic area up against his and get off that way. "It takes me a little while to come that way, so I just have to make sure that he can last long enough," she says. "There's nothing more annoying than when I'm about to get off and he comes right before me."

Now, you may have been surprised to see that only 30 percent of women said this was their favorite position. For years we've been reading that woman on top is the favored position among women. All the magazines say the same thing. But among the women I talked to, a lot of them didn't like it simply because it was too much work. Have I touched on what a lazy bunch of bitches women can be?

"I'm *way* too lazy to get on top most of the

time," said a friend of mine, who is lazy not only in the sack but also in real life, preferring to sleep till noon when possible and avoiding both full-time jobs and full-time relationships. She is one of the few women I know who told her long-term boyfriend that she would be happy if they could demote their relationship status to just sleeping together after he asked if they could move in together.

"All that energy of bouncing up and down and trying to look sexy, it honestly makes me too tired to get off," she said. I had to laugh. Sometimes it's just better when you don't have to get a workout to reach an orgasm. Why do you think the orgasm machine was invented and beloved by lazy women so much? Still, other women don't like it just because they think they look funky from that angle.

"I hate thinking that he can just see my pooch and my saggy boobs dangling over him when I'm on top," said Sarah, a twenty-seven-year-old student. "I get too self-conscious to have a good time. It's OK when the lights are out, but I prefer to be lying on my back so my stomach looks flat. Even though I have to squeeze my elbows in to keep the boobs from flopping off to the sides too much."

Missionary

Poor missionary gets a bad name. Everyone thinks it's the boring position. Even the name sounds like something that unattractive, chaste Mormons do during their awkward reproductive years. There's no oomph or excitement surrounding it, but this is totally misleading. Missionary is actually awesome, and according to most of the women I talked to, it is their favorite position. Partly because they don't have to break a sweat by doing any of the pumping action, but also because it is the one in which they feel closest to their partners, and they can feel them deep inside but without any of the pain that comes with other deep positions (more on those in a bit).

"I like it best because I get to put my arms around my boyfriend's neck and bring him in for a kiss during and afterward, and there's something sexy about seeing a sweaty guy on top of you. I especially love watching his O face, and knowing right when he's about to get off," said Sarah. "I can decide if I want him to go ahead and go for it, or if I want him to slow down and try and let me catch up." This intrigued me—she was saying she often let her boyfriend go ahead and come even if she had no intention of doing so, something I suspected most women did, even if a lot of them said they got off every time.

"So you don't always come?" I asked her.

"Oh, God no, do you?"

I shook my head. Of course, not always, especially during quickies, which were basically invented for dudes. Women don't do a whole lot of things quickly—showering, shopping—and orgasms are no exception.

"I'd say I actually come about fifty percent of the time we're doing it," she said. "And it's not a bad thing, like he's not bad in bed or anything. He's great. It just takes me a little while and sometimes I don't care if I do or not, like if I'd rather sleep or just am feeling generous and want to get him off and be happy. It still always feels good. I think that's one thing men just can't understand, how it still feels good for us even when we don't come. It doesn't work that way for them."

I nodded. Sometimes I am really hell bent on having a nice solid orgasm and an even nicer deep sleep afterward, but sometimes I just want my guy to get off and give me a kiss goodnight. It's never a reflection on his talents. Because I've never been one to fake it (after that one relationship where I ended up having to do it for about two years). I just usually never make a big deal about it. And neither does he. Things get tricky when the guy is always asking, "Did you come? Why not? Did I do something wrong? I don't understand why you didn't come. Let me make you come." That's when they're inviting a faker into bed with them. However, I digress. I was discussing the solid and awesome missionary position. At the end of the day, missionary is a sure-fire winner—especially with a couple of twists added to it.

"I like to slide a pillow under my ass when we're doing missionary," said Jackie, a thirty-year-old editor. "I read about it years ago in *Cosmo* or something, and it actually really works in making things feel different and better for me," she said. "It is a little deeper, so if you don't need that then don't bother, but I think I might have a really long vagina or something. I'm always down for deeper."

Another woman told me she likes it because she can move her legs into various positions to switch things up each time: "Sometimes they're on his shoulders, sometimes just spread out to the sides. Sometimes one leg is up, the other around his back. It's never boring," she told me. "Also, it makes it easier for his mouth to remain on my boobs, which is key to getting me off."

One woman told me she had a really different reason for loving the good, old man on top. "I can easily reach around and stroke his ass and cup his balls, which is my secret weapon, especially if I've decided I've had enough or I've already come. One or two strokes under there and he's done for." I knew what she was talking about. There's not a man in the world who doesn't like testicular action during sex.

Doggy Style

Whenever I'm looking to swing around into this position, I never, ever say, "Wanna do it doggy style?" I always say "Let's do it from behind," or something similar. The term *doggy style* grosses me out. Maybe I've seen too many nasty little dog boners in my life. That's not to say the position itself does—done right, it's simply awesome. However, for a lot of women, it's just too deep, and it actually hurts.

"The only reason doggy style is bearable is because dudes come really quickly from it so we don't have to suffer too long," said one of my most cynical friends. "It hurts my ovaries or something! I can't handle it for more than a few minutes. It's just *too* deep." Another friend of mine said, "There's not a woman alive that can handle that kind of pounding for ten minutes. It makes you sore inside and out. I feel like I can feel his penis poking out the front of my stomach. Not hot!"

One of my friends took the opposite stance. She said the position made her feel sexiest and most porn like. "I know my ass looks OK from that angle, and there's something animalistic and awesome about him grabbing onto it with both hands while we're having sex," she said. "It also frees my hands to work on myself, either with fingers or vibrator, so I can get off at the same time. I don't usually come from penetration alone, and I don't think that's the best position for that anyway, since there's no friction on the clit area."

One thing everyone agrees on is that the name for it is stupid. "Can we please petition to change that term?" said one of my friends. "I have a dog, and I watch her hump her toys and my pillows and it grosses me out. I don't need to think about that when I'm trying to come." Woof.

Sideways

I haven't met a single woman who likes this so-called spooning sexual position. "How is he supposed to get it in and keep it there?" asked one. "Every time you make any kind of sliding move, it pops out and you have to try and bend it back in. There's not face-to-face action, so no kissing or anything. It's just annoying."

I have read all too many articles in men's magazines that extol the wonders of this position and claim that women love the kind of penetration you can get from it—but it's bullshit. No one likes it. Seriously, given a list of ten ways to do it, this one should be dead last. Spooning is for afterward. The only time this position is appropriate is when it's super early in the morning and the guy has a boner digging into your back and is so turned on that he sticks it in. "I actually like it when my boyfriend does that from time to time," said one friend. "It makes me feel sexy that he has to satisfy his morning wood there and then. But if we were going to bed and about to do it, there is no way in hell I'd ever roll on my side and offer up the spooning position. And he'd be like, 'What the fuck, are you going to sleep?'"

Sixty-nine

Sixty-nine made us laugh a lot when we were in middle school, and we tried it in high school, but now we rarely do it on a regular basis, even though it can feel really good. Why aren't most women into it? Again, too much work! Some women also said that it made it hard for them to concentrate on how good it actually felt to have a guy go down on them when they were all bent up in weird ways and trying to give a decent blow job at the same time.

"I've actually enjoyed it as a kind of sexy foreplay thing, but when it comes to actually getting off from it, it's a no go," said one woman. "If it starts to feel super good, I have to stop what I'm doing to him and lie there and let myself go ahead and have the orgasm," she said. "Then I feel bad because I neglected his dick."

"Too crampy for me," said another girl. "It just gives me a huge pain in the neck to force my head forward like that when I'm all bent over. Though my ATM pin is still 6969, since I chose it back when I was eighteen and that was the funniest number in the world back then."

"Sixty-nine, dude!" another simply said before collapsing into laughter. I realized, not for the first time, that my friends were seriously immature, especially because if they were referencing Bill and Ted, they were in their early thirties.

Dirty Talk

Talking dirty is one of the best ways to get things turned up a notch in the sack with most Dirty Girls. All the women I've talked to like a little verbal action between the sheets to get even more turned on, but there's usually a slight problem when it comes to talking nasty—it can be really embarrassing, especially if we're not sure how well it'll be received. And, of course, a guy has to be super careful about what he says to a chick in bed when she's naked and vulnerable.

"You are making me so hard," is good for most women. "I am thinking of a sister sandwich between you and Lisa—how hot is that?" is not. All women have a case of dirty talk gone wrong, and mostly it was the guys at fault. But women can say things that men don't want to hear, either.

"I was dirty talking with my boyfriend, and we had upped the usual stuff and gotten really filthy one night and were talking about how we wanted to have a threesome and group sex and go to a sex club and watch each other have sex with strangers. Real nasty stuff," a girlfriend of mine told me. "In the heat of it all, and honestly because it's what I was actually thinking about, I said something about him getting butt fucked by a woman with a strap-on while he had sex with me. I thought it was hot! Apparently he didn't—he stopped midstroke and climbed off and went into the guest room for like an hour." She couldn't figure out what was wrong, and when he finally came out, he told her that just because he had fantasies about group sex, it didn't mean he was gay in any way. Anyway, the whole thing was awful, and we didn't have sex again for days. We certainly never talked like that again."

Another close friend of mine said she accidentally hurt her boyfriend's feelings by talking about a huge giant cock while they were doing it: "We were whispering dirty things to each other, and I said something about how good it would feel to have another huge, hard cock in me at the same time, and he suddenly got all whimpery and stopped. When I asked what was wrong, he said that it sucked he didn't satisfy me because he was too small. Give me a break!"

"Well, was he too small?" I couldn't help but ask.

"No, he was fine. It's just that it was a legit fantasy of mine to have two guys in me at once. But I'll never say that to a dude again."

My favorite case of dirty talk gone wrong is from a friend of mine, a real perv of a chick who in a way is every man's fantasy because she's always up for everything sexually (she even claims to enjoy butt sex), and she is always the first to give in to a fantasy request, whether handcuffs or a facial. One night, as she was going to town with a new guy, the talk started getting heated, and she whipped out one of the lines her and an ex used to enjoy.

"Tell me I'm a slut, your dirty little whore," she said as he was pounding away on top. Aghast, he immediately stopped and curled up into a ball. "I can't believe you'd subject yourself to that kind of treatment from a man," he said, horrified and disturbed. She suddenly did feel like that dirty whore she wanted him to call her. She watched as he got dressed.

"I think you might have some really bad father issues," he told her. "I'm sorry, but I don't think it's healthy for you to say things like that. I don't think I want to stay here." He left.

"This is a week after I had another guy do the

switcheroo and suddenly stick it in my butt," she told me. "So you never know what you're getting in the sack. I guess it was sweet he was sensitive, but I don't have dad issues. I just think it's hot to role play and get really gross and say weird things sometimes. Or maybe I do have dad issues. Great."

HAVE YOUR MAN READ THIS, PLEASE: WHAT NOT TO SAY IN BED

One time I was in the middle of a romp when my then boyfriend said something about how he would love to see another guy have sex with me. I was totally taken aback—didn't most guys loathe the idea of being cheated on and having someone else have sex with their girlfriends? Did this mean he didn't love me or respect me? I felt dirty, sad, and truly upset. The next day I looked online at that fantasy to see what it meant. Some analysts said that a guy who says this would be afraid of being cuckolded and would rather be aware of his girlfriend having sex with another guy. Others said there was a possibility he was gay. I decided to go with the former analysis. And then I got over it and got into the idea of it, strictly as part of our fantasy and dirty-talk routine. But men need to know that some things will just never be kosher in bed. Here are ten of them:

1. *Sister, brother, mother.* Anything involving another family member is taboo, not to

mention incestuous and deeply gross. Keep it to yourself.

2. *Best friends or roommates.* No woman wants you to bring up her sexy best friend when she's having sex with you, even if you're thinking about it. You're risking not only tears and total anger but also a ruined friendship. And you don't need that on your plate, especially if you'd like to continue to see the best friend and fantasize about her.

3. *Another dude.* A lot of women have told me they sometimes wonder whether their boyfriends and husbands are secretly gay. So don't stoke the fire by bringing another dude into your dirty talk. If he's strictly pleasuring the woman in this verbal fantasy, then maybe, but if you describe his boner in rapt joy, we're gonna go to the toilet and cry—and know that we were right about you and your homosexual tendencies!

4. *Animals.* Leave Fido out of dirty talk, even if you do think it would feel nice to have him lick your balls. It's illegal, farm boy.

5. *Poo*. No woman likes scat when it comes to sex. Those perverts who get off from Cleveland steamers and other fecal matters are always men. Have you heard of a woman who likes someone to take a dump on her chest? No, because she does not exist. So don't bring up poo—or pee, for that matter. Golden showers are weird and gross.

6. *Rape.* I did a *Maxim* column on this, and a psychotherapist told me that while a lot of woman fantasize about "rape," it's not real rape they're thinking of—it's about letting themselves be submissive. In real life, rape is awful, scary, and about power, not sex. So never, ever bring up that term in bed or while role playing.

7. *Celebs*. I don't care if you're Team Aniston or Team Jolie—leave the chicks who have highly unattainable beauty and bodies out of our bedroom.

8. *Blood, mutilation, and so on.* Yes, there are a lot of women and men who are into this kind of thing, but something tells me they're not the ones reading this book.

The average chick would freak out if a guy said something like, "I want to cut you and lick the blood off your tits." Holy murderer, get the eff off of us or we're calling the cops.

9. *"I want you to have my baby."* OK, so this one depends. Some women are trying to conceive and might think this is cute or something. But I once had a guy say this to me in the middle of coitus, and it scared the hell out of me. Mainly because we'd only started sleeping together. I wriggled out from underneath him so damn quickly he never even got another poke in. Men, it is not hot to talk about conception when we have zero desire to have a baby with you or anyone else, for that matter. Don't assume every woman thinks that children are simply adorable.

10. *"You are a disgusting whore."* With the exception of my pervy friend who liked being called a dirty slut, for most women, the term *whore* is totally loaded. We had to deal with bitches in high school calling us whores, with our moms warning us not

to be sluts, with the church we grew up in scaring us with tales of harlots who hung at the gallows. Don't ever throw *slut* or *whore* at a woman in bed unless she has brought it up first. Also, the c word. *Cunt* is unacceptable to say to a girl, either in bed or outside of it, at any time. A guy once called me that when we were arguing at a bar. I dropped my pint of beer into his lap and threw the glass at his head. We eventually made up, but he learned not to drop the c word on me again.

Chapter Nine

When Dirty Girls Fall In Love—And When They Fall Out of It

When it comes to falling in and out of love, I've found that women and men are pretty equal. Where we've had it wrong is assuming that all women are pining for someone to love them and that men are doing their best to avoid getting sucked into a relationship. That's bullshit.

Some men and women are addicted to love, and it's quite easy for them to meet someone new and immediately fall in love and be in relationship after relationship after relationship (we all know people who can't be single). From what I've discovered, these people are not that great at taking care of themselves when they're left to their own devices, and they hate feeling lonely. They become addicted to that euphoric feeling that new love presents. It's stronger than crack.

Then there are those who are cynical about the whole thing, and they tend to be overly picky and find serious flaws with every single person they meet. They *want* to find someone they like (or can at least tolerate), but it's hard because no one ever lives up to their incredibly high standards.

Women (and Dudes) Who Fall In Love Too Easily

I have a Dirty Girl friend who enjoys men and partying with equal vigor, but she has a problem— she tends to get seriously into certain guys too quickly. By the second date, she has told everyone she knows about him, and she says things like, "I really think this is the one. He is so cute and funny, and he's tall, and we would have really cute babies together because I'm on the short side so it would be a great balance." I always want to tell her that she's being a little overzealous (OK, psycho) and to be careful, but I usually go with something more tactful, like, "Well, take it slowly! You don't want to rush things!" But she *loves* rushing things. And it's nearly inevitable that when something burns really bright and fast, it burns out bright and fast. Not to mention, I think she scares the crap out of most men because she's such an eager beaver.

"He turned out to be such an asshole!" she said last time it happened, crying into her drink and smoking furiously.

"What did he do?" I asked.

"I asked if he wanted to come over and watch a movie, and he said he had a dinner with friends and couldn't but that he'd text me afterward. Then he never texted me, even though I texted him. Then he finally emailed the next day and he said he was going upstate for the weekend and he'd be in touch when he was back, so I asked what he was doing upstate and he just said visiting some friends, and then I looked on his Facebook and saw that some girl who writes to him a lot lives upstate. So I know he's visiting her and he's lying to me and not texting. What an asshole!"

"And how long have you been hanging out?" I asked.

"We hung out three times last week, two nights in a row," she sniffed. "I thought it was really going somewhere."

I try to tell women like this that they can't get

too excited about dudes too quickly. And I say this from experience, not because I'm some kind of relationship guru. I once met a guy on an airplane who I thought was such a great match—and a great catch. I was in college and returning from visiting my sister in New York. This tall, cute guy sat next to me, and we immediately smiled at each other and started chatting. We talked the whole flight, drinking and laughing and having a great time. He told me he was opening a nightclub in Boston and that he came from a wealthy New England family. He told me all about a fabulous restaurant in San Francisco that I needed to try and about this excellent show playing at a little theater he thought I'd love. By the time we landed, I was seriously into him. I gave him my number, and he called me the very next night to make a date to go to the show and to dinner. I was ecstatic. Up until then the guys I'd gone on dates with in college included a heroin junkie who told me he was reformed but obviously wasn't, a guy I picked up at the coffee shop I worked at who shaved his back, and a guy who ended up being gay. Not an awesome run. I got so excited, I even told my parents about the guy, and they were so excited for me my mom actually said, "Well, tell him we say hello." What, is that not a hot first date line or something?

Our date went pretty well, but something seemed amiss that I couldn't quite put my finger on. I think it was that he told me he was working at Nordstrom as a manager in the men's department, trying to get some practice as a manager because he was going to be managing the nightclub he was opening with some friends. But he took me out, paid for everything, and we had a generally nice time. We even made out. So I told all my friends about him and declared I thought I'd met someone really special and great.

Our next date was to see the movie *Crouching Tiger, Hidden Dragon*. When I got there, he had a bag of Burger King in hand.

"Sorry, I'm starving," he said, wolfing down two Whoppers while I waited for him to chow down. I mentioned that I thought we'd go to dinner afterward, and he said something about being broke. During the movie, he put his feet up on the seat in front of him, dropped his legs open to a spread eagle, and farted—loudly, and consistently. I actually asked him to please stop farting because they reeked, and he cackled with laughter. Weird, this perfect guy was turning out to be annoying! I decided to give it one more shot, and our third and last date was at a bar. He asked me to meet him at a swanky little martini bar, and I was excited. I got dressed up in a sexy number and waited for him at the bar, sipping on a martini. Then I had another. He was more than thirty minutes late. I felt like a loser and, even though the bartender was being kind and talking to me, was about to hightail it out of there when he waltzed in and ordered a double martini. I paid for it. He seemed kind of drunk, and when I asked where he'd been, he said nowhere. Then he asked if I wanted to see something cool. He grabbed my hand, took me outside, and dropped his pants. He was wearing maroon bikini briefs.

"Isn't my underwear sexy?" he asked, pants around his ankles on the street. I never saw him again. Oh, wait, I lie. I saw him in the shoe department at Nordstrom, where I guess he was actually a shoe salesman. And years later, he came to a restaurant I was waiting tables at, remembered me, and totally tried to hit on me. He was still selling shoes and told me to come by and see him at Nordstrom anytime.

The moral of the story is this: don't get fixated on a dude after one or two dates. And never go traveling with a guy when you've only just met. I had a friend who met a guy, had a weeklong whirlwind romance with him, and decided to go on a romantic beach vacation by the following weekend. It was a disaster. To get stuck in an awkward situation with someone at a local restaurant or bar is one thing—to be in Barbados with him when he makes you get up early on Sunday to go to church is quite another.

The reality of love and dating is that there are a ton of men out there who get too excited too quickly about someone new and gross her out instead of exciting her back. A friend of mine recently met a guy and really liked him. Things had started off swimmingly, except from the first day he wrote emails like, "I can't believe a woman like you is still single! You are so perfect. How lucky am I that we met?" She thought it was cute at first. I thought it was a tad creepy and kind of wondered what was wrong with him. "Really, is anything wrong with you?" he asked her on their second date. "I've never dated anyone like you before, and I've never felt so strongly about someone so quickly. I feel like I want to get married!" This made her see my side of things a little bit more. When he started to refer to her only as Honey Buns and had picked out baby names for their future child by the third date, she couldn't deal anymore. She told him she still had feelings for her ex and that she thought they'd be getting back together. The guy was crushed, and she felt terrible, until he started Facebook stalking her and then sent angry texts about how lame it was that she had blocked him from her Facebook page.

"It literally makes me want to vomit now, thinking back to having sex with him and thinking that this could be something great," she says.

It's hard not to get excited when you're dating someone new and you really like them and they seem to like you back, but things are just not always what they seem. I once had great conversation with a guy at a bar all night, kissed him outside as he walked me to a cab, and then met up with him the following week for lunch. We were having a great lunch date when he mentioned something about taking his wife's grandmother to a retirement home that weekend. "You're married?" I asked, kind of shocked. I don't know why I hadn't thought to look at his hand to see if he was wearing a ring. I certainly noticed it just then. "Yeah," he said. "Is that OK?"

The Boyfriend Girl: Women Who Always Have Boyfriends Are Usually the Hottest Messes

Full disclosure: I *like* having boyfriends. I always have, from the first time I got my taste of a real one senior year of high school. I fell so in love with a long-haired, stoner hipster who had a silver Saab 900 and always carried a bag of weed. We spent every waking moment together after school, canoodling and smoking cigarettes and listening to the Beastie Boys while we drove around, and then we'd make out in his bed. I was so happy (as long as I was with him) and so unhappy when we were apart that I knew it was real, true love and he felt the same. Well, like most high school romances, this one eventually died, but I'd gotten my taste of what it was like to need, to be needed, to want, to be wanted, to yearn for someone so much that it hurt. I fell in love with love, and I spent a great amount of time trying to get that same heart-lifting and heart-wrenching feeling back. It was official—I was a *relationship* kind of girl.

Unfortunately, the universe had different plans for me, and I spent a good couple of years not coming remotely close to being in love or in a decent relationship, but I eventually found a new one and it was great. The best part for me was waking up together on weekends, making eggs and pancakes, and then getting back into bed to do the crossword together and have morning sex. Then we'd venture outside, wander around until it was time for dinner, eat, go to a bar and get drunk, sometimes go do karaoke, and then go back to bed. It was all so great. Until it stopped being so great, and it started to actually bore me a little bit. At that point, I started to fantasize a bit about this other guy I knew, and I started mentally straying from my great relationship. When we finally ended, I very quickly found out what it was like to kiss the other guy and immediately dated him for a little while. Then I moved cities, but I already had someone lined up in the new town. When that guy and I broke up, I was ready to be single and enjoy life as a single girl again, but then a friend I drunkenly made out with one night started becoming a regular hookup and soon thereafter became my boyfriend. I was in love again, and all of my friends found me highly annoying.

"Dude, you always have to have a boyfriend!" they told me.

"No, I don't," I protested. "I didn't plan for it to be this way—it's just how it works out timing-wise."

"No, you can't handle being alone," they said. "You are codependent and needy and hate not having someone around."

Maybe this was kind of true. I did prefer having a boyfriend, but I liked what came with that—regular sex and a regular partner to do things with on the weekends, like go out of town and have regular sex. The fact that my boyfriends had overlapped so closely was a bummer, but what are you going to do? I certainly wasn't going to break up with one of them just to prove a point to people that, yes, I could be alone.

Truth be told, when I'm alone I'm kind of a hot mess who eats toast for dinner and drinks too much then I wake up feeling crappy. You know how there are those dudes who you're friends with who are major alcoholics and always smell kind of bad because they have BO and booze coming out of their pores in the mornings? Or how their clothes are always wrinkly, and you know they don't eat right or take great care of themselves? Women are always saying, "He just needs to get himself a girlfriend," not "He needs to go to rehab or AA, start bathing more and washing his clothes, and cooking healthy dinners for one. He needs to appreciate being alone! He doesn't know how to be alone!" Nope, dude needs a chick to take care of him. So why can't women need dudes to take care of them, or at least help them stop being such alcoholic sloths? I think we all need someone to help us be a better person. For me, boyfriends are just that. They make me want to be a better woman—or at least put my clothes away on hangers and cook dishes that include at least one vegetable from time to time. Most Dirty Girls I know are better in relationships simply because it makes them care enough to try and appear un-dirty.

The Picky Girl

I got a message from my older sister the other day who wanted to tell me all about the date she went on with this new guy that she'd met at a party in LA. "I have to tell you all about it. Call me as soon as you can!" she left on my voicemail. I was excited, thinking it must have gone well.

I called her back as soon as I could. "Well? Tell me all about it!"

"Well, he's really hot, really cool, he works at a

sweet ad agency, and he's funny. He took me to the Hollywood Bowl, and we had the best time, and then we totally made out at the end of it," she said.

"Wow, that sounds perfect!" I said. "Are you excited about him?"

"Ick. No," she said. "He also unfortunately had a spastic tic and kissed like an eighth grader. So fer-git it!" she laughed. I was disappointed. I'd wanted this story to have a Hollywood rom-com ending.

"Are you *sure* he had a spastic tic?" I asked, thinking, well, you can always teach a guy to kiss.

"Gillian," she said. "I counted the seconds between each spaz. It was every thirty seconds. It was a definite spastic tic in his shoulder."

"Oh, well, then," I said. "Fer-git it!"

Ah, women. For all their bitching and moaning about how they can't find a good man, most of them are just as quick to shut down a guy who has a flaw he can't control as a frat boy who just found out his Tri-Delt date to the Spring Fling is nicknamed Cankles. That's the irony when it comes to relationships and men and women—men often think women are totally desperate, but the reality is far different. Sure, women want to meet someone they love being around and can have fun with. Don't men? But during the dating and sex days, women can, and tend to be, just as dicky as dudes—guys call this bat-shit crazy.

I've heard countless horror stories from women who have gone on dates that were horribly, horribly wrong. Their terror tales range from him being too short, to him not having enough money to pay to get his car fixed and so she had to drive him everywhere, to him trying to stick it in her pooper on the very first night in the sack.

But, mostly, women are a picky bunch of bitches, and it's very often the perpetually single ones who are the worst. My friends and I have a name for this: the dreads. That's when something seemingly innocent can turn a chick off so quickly that the idea of seeing the guy again can actually make her physically ill. The dreads vary among women. I know one girl who could never look at a certain guy again after she saw the dorky way he ran for the bus, and another who dumped her boyfriend of a few months after he looked her in the eye in the sack and solemnly said, "I want to pepper your belly with kisses."

"Do you realize how disgusting that was?" she asked me.

"Yes. Yes, I do," I assured her. Cheesy lines,

especially ones cribbed from movies, are the quickest way to get out of a woman's heart. We can overlook beer bellies and bald heads and bad tribal tattoos if we really like a guy. Well, some of us can. But once he opens his mouth and says, "I could spend the entire night with you softly stroking my hair," it's dreads city. And we're outta there.

My friend Ginny is like this—she's no slouch, and guys often show interest in her, but they say or do one thing that she finds unattractive, and then she's got the major dreads and begins hatching her exit strategy.

Last time we spoke, I asked her about the new guy she'd been dating, who seemed to have serious potential—good job, never married, lived in the same city, single, and looking for a girlfriend.

"Ugh, not good. I'm trying to figure out whether I should dump him now or wait until I've met someone else," she said.

"Why, what happened?" I cried. "I thought you really liked him and he was a good match."

"I did, but then you should have seen his Facebook status updates," she said. "They are so idiotic, I can't stand it. It makes me sick to even look at him now," she says.

"You're dumping him over his Facebook status updates?" I asked. "Isn't that a little bit mean? And can't you overlook it?"

"No, you don't understand, I tried. But he's also a serious constant updater, so they're not only embarrassing, but there are new ones up there all day long for me to barf at." She emailed a few of the worst ones:

MATT FERNANDEZ thinks life is wonderful, and if you don't stop to look around once in a while, you could miss it!

MATT FERNANDEZ says smile and the whole world smiles with you.

MATT FERNANDEZ tummy hurts, too much ice cream :p!

"Errr. Yeah, that's actually a problem," I said.

"He also baby talks. All the time," she said.

"OK, so your dilemma is whether to wait until you've found someone else to dump him?" I asked. "I say go ahead and do it now. Baby talk should never be tolerated."

"I knew you'd come around."

And then there are those women who are picky over physical attributes, whether they refuse to date a ginger or a guy who is shorter than them. I have a friend who is adamantly opposed to dating men who are not of a certain height, even if they seem great in every other way.

"So you're saying you refuse to be set up with this guy who is an executive producer of prime-time TV shows because you heard he was a little short?" I asked her once.

"Everyone has their thing," she said. "Mine is short guys. They will never do it for me, no matter how wonderful they are otherwise," she said.

"I think that's ridiculous," I said. "You really need to be more open-minded."

"OK, well, would you date a guy whose penis was three inches under what you usually liked?" She had me there.

The Bitterly Single Woman

There are plenty of women who never fall in love, and it's not because they are heinously unattractive. There are a million reasons certain women seem to always be single, and just like the girl who falls in love too quickly or always has a boyfriend, they can also be annoying. Going too long without kisses or cuddling or sex makes anyone—no matter how independent and fabulous—pretty grumpy. So why are there so many single women out there, even though they are actively seeking a boyfriend? From what I've noticed, it's mainly because they either are really picky or have seriously bad taste and judgment when it comes to liking a guy. Maybe I shouldn't say *bad* taste—maybe it's that they tend to have overly ambitious taste when it comes to the kind of guys they are attracted to. They always fall hard for that guy who is, for lack of a better term, out of their league.

It is because of these high standards that many women stay single for a long time. Some Dirty Girls live in a fantasy world, where Ryan Reynolds, a sweet guy who loves to surf and cook and play with babies and works in a cool creative job and makes good money but isn't ostentatious about it, is looking for a woman just like them—and he's always just around the corner, right, so why not hold out a little bit?

I once tried to explain to my friend that maybe she needed to lower her standards a little bit, and that maybe then she'd find someone she was really into, even though he wasn't perfect.

"I refuse to 'settle,' for anything or anyone," she told me. "I know what I want, and I know that I can find it, even if it takes me longer than most people. Even if I never do—at least I won't be settling." You have to admire her conviction. Come to think of it, I do know an awful lot of women in relationships who are perpetually complaining about their mates, to the point that you wonder why they were really with them at all. So maybe holding out for Ryan Reynolds wasn't such a bad move after all.

HAVE YOUR MAN READ THIS, PLEASE: HOW NOT TO GIVE A WOMAN THE DREADS

It's not that all women are picky, bitchy assholes who won't like or respect you if you're not perfect. We're not that crazy at the end of the day. We actually really *like* it if you have flaws, especially because it makes us feel less insecure about our own little flaws. Your poochy stomach? Most of us think it's cute. Got a hairy back? So fucking what? As long as you are into us and are fun and respectful, then there's really not a whole lot about you that is going to turn us off. Of course, when women are in love, they are generally blind to most everything that could be considered faults anyway.

However, when you are newly dating someone, it's tricky territory. If everything was going well and then suddenly she never wants to see you again, you have probably given her the dreads. Here are a few surefire ways to gross her out, according to women I have asked.

1. *Cheesy lines or baby talk.* I know firsthand how gross this is. I once spent the night with a guy, and in the morning he woke up, made coffee, and called out, "Sweetie poo? Do you like milk?" I froze, not sure what to do after being called "sweetie poo" by a veritable stranger. It gave me the dreads.

2. *Revealing your dorky secrets too soon.* I once dated a guy who was into the *Sound of Music* soundtrack as much as I was. But by the time we discovered our shared passion for the "Lonely Goatherd," we were in a solid relationship already. Had he tried to play it for me on the first date, I would have probably walked away.

3. *Not taking care of blemishes.* One of my friends said she recently went on a date with a guy who had a big whitehead on his chin and just let it be. Throughout the whole meal, she didn't know where to look. "I wanted to reach out and squeeze it," she said. "It was horrible."

4. *Not handling your liquor.* This is a big one. No woman thinks a puker is sexy or cool.

Again, if you're in a secure relationship with someone, you can puke and shit your pants at the same time and she'll take care of you, but when it's early days, being that guy who drinks too much and gets sick is really unattractive.

5. *Bad kissing*. If you're old enough to be dating, you shouldn't be a bad kisser. To us, bad kissers equals bad in bed. It's not hard to be a good kisser: just go slow (but not too slow; that's also gross) and don't ever dart your tongue in and out of her mouth. Bad kissing is the ultimate dread for all women, and there's not much you can do to redeem yourself from it.

Chapter Ten

The End Game

How Dirty Girls Really Feel
about Happily Ever After

*M*ost Dirty Girls think that they want to eventually get married and have babies (or at least just get married) in their lifetime. Even if the timing isn't now, they think that this is how things will end up somewhere down the line when asked to envision their future. Because that's just the way the world seems to work—there are a series of steps that we take throughout life until the inevitable doomsday: Shady Pines Retirement Home. It's also the way women are naturally made. We all harbor a nurturing instinct—yes, even you, you cynical bitch. You might think kids smell like barf and couldn't possibly be more annoying, but if you came across a weak and thirsty kitten on the side of the road, you would probably stop to help the poor little thing. The urge to protect the weak and the cute is too hard to resist. Oh, yeah, and there's that whole regular sex and feeling secure that we have someone to lean on in the good and bad times thing that's pretty appealing too. And everyone abhors the idea of growing old alone. You'd be a freak to declare that you want to die old and alone.

Even though half of us women are children of divorce and most of us have been in therapy because of it, and we know the marriage statistics that at least 50 percent of marriages will fail (and it often doesn't seem like women married with kids are any happier or more fulfilled than women without a husband and kids), we're still not deterred from this whole marriage business for some reason. We want our shot at the grown-up things in life too. Who knows—maybe *we* won't make a mess of it. Maybe *we* won't get divorced and screw up our kids and annoy them to the point that they vow to never be like us. Doubtful, but we want our fair chance at this grand life step, and we deserve it. Plus, life is hard. We work our asses off and still get paid less than men for doing the exact same job. Sports dominate the TV schedule for most of the year. We have to keep our pubes nice and trim so we can get regular oral sex. So we should be able to get dressed up and beautiful and have people buy us presents and give us all sorts of love and attention at least one day out of our life on our wedding day. And let's not forget that weddings can be serious fun. All of your friends and family are in one place, the booze is flowing, and terrible dancers are cutting loose and entertaining you. What's not to love? Unless, of course, you don't actually love the groom, which, sadly, happens more often than it should.

Dirty Girls and Marriage

Even though shitty marriages are still arranged in a lot of parts of the world, would *anyone* trust her freaking parents to pick out a suitable husband? If I'd let my mom and dad have any say in whom I ended up with, I'd have married the blond golf pro in pleated khakis who gives lessons at their country club. A lifetime of free swing tips? Totally worth the hand of their third-born daughter! A lot of modern Dirty Girls still marry the wrong guy just because they feel that it's expected of them by a certain age or because they feel some sort of pressure to check that milestone off their life list before they're past the age of marriage eligibility. The average age for marriage in the United States is now twenty-six for women and twenty-seven for men. Of course, this depends on where you live—in my hometown of New York City it's between thirty and thirty-five. I don't know any women who were married at twenty-six, but I sure knew a lot of twenty-six-year-olds who were psyched to have $3 PBRs with me at 3 a.m. on a work night.

But I don't think the age thing is as big of a deal as the rest of it is. If you're going to get married, first and foremost, you have to really *like* your future husband, enough that you're not mapping out your divorce or your future affairs with hot co-workers before you've even finalized your bridal party. Divorce is a nice option if the whole operation turns out to be totally sucky, but it's really not the goal. A huge problem with a lot of marriages is that the bride already knows going into it that her heart isn't truly there. She might be so fixated on the idea of a wedding and a husband that she's less fixated on the dude himself and what it might mean to actually wake up with his ass day in and day out for the rest of her life. And that's where a lot of problems begin. I know three different couples whose marriages ended in under a year—and all of the women said that they kind of knew they were being foolish about getting hitched as they were going in for dress fittings.

"I knew before I was getting married that it was a bad idea," says thirty-year-old Sam. "But we'd been together for three years which seemed like the right amount of time, we'd lived together for two of them, and he was a nice guy who wanted to marry me. Or maybe he just felt like it was time too." Right around the time her boyfriend was putting down ring payments, she struck up a serious flirtation with an old colleague, inviting him out for drinks with the intention of making out with him, just to do something different and wild before she got engaged.

"I knew he was picking out the ring because one of his friends had let it slip one night," she says. "And instead of jumping up and down with joy, I bugged out and wanted to make out with someone totally inappropriate instead," she says. "Not exactly a great sign that you're ready to make a long-term commitment to someone." When her boyfriend did propose a month later, Sam of course said yes and pretended to be excited about it for a few months. "I just kept finding myself more and more in contact with the old colleague, and we met and I made out with him on a regular basis during lunch, even though I thought having a ring on my finger would make me commit wholly and stop being such a bitch." It didn't happen, and neither did the wedding. "I couldn't go through with it, especially not after I started having legit serious feelings for the other dude, even though I probably just used that as an excuse not to get sucked into the wedding," she says. "I'd look at myself in the mirror when I was brushing my teeth and just go, 'What the fuck are you doing?'" she says. She broke up with her fiancé and went through a horrible year of trying to piece her life back together after she'd been on the so-called right track.

"Some days I thought I'd made a horrible mistake and maybe it would have been worth it to just go ahead and get married instead of being thirty and alone and lonely and lost," she says. "But then I think about the inevitable divorce, and how I just headed things off at the pass. I fooled around with the other dude for a little bit at first, but then I realized I wasn't into him as a rebound. Now I'm single and dating and actually really enjoying everything.

I want to get married someday but just not to the wrong guy. I don't regret any of it, though I know a lot of women would have just gone ahead and gone through with it rather than face the pain and drama of breaking off an engagement and crushing someone else."

Another friend of mine is completely wary about marriage, mainly because she's petrified of complete and utter monogamy. "I've always ended my relationships because I found myself attracted to someone else after a while," she says. "What if that happens when I get married? It's a sobering thought—to be with one guy sexually for the rest of my life? Will that ever be enough for me?"

I checked in with some of my married pals to ask how they knew someone was marriage material or, at the very least, not the wrong guy.

"My husband was successful enough in his own creative way that he wouldn't ever be resentful or jealous of my own success in my own creative way," said one of them. "That's one of the most important things in the world to me—that I can have a job or career that I like and is stimulating, even if it doesn't always pay really well, and he'll always, always be supportive of that. Nothing is less attractive than a guy who is either unsupportive of your work or is jealous of what you do."

Agreed! I once dated a guy who was having a very hard time in his career, and as supportive as I was, listening to him and helping him with suggestions on how to improve things and being there for him whenever he needed it, it was never enough. I'd "never understand" what he was going through as a man. During this time, I'd also just happened to land my dream job. My dream job paid shit, but it was fun and cool and I'd been in these crappy dead-end gigs as an assistant to total ass wipes for three years prior. I thought the new job was well deserved—I seriously welcomed it, at the very least. I went out for drinks with my boyfriend after my first day at work to tell him all about it, and I was absolutely buoyant. I was talking a mile a minute about the people I worked with and how much I liked them already, and how my boss had me sit in the big meetings with all the senior editors and welcomed my input and said one of my ideas was good—and how I'd gotten free tickets to go see a cool concert the next day, one of the great perks of working at this fantastic magazine. My boyfriend sat stone-faced and listened to me go off happily, and when I finally slowed down, he snapped at me.

"I'm happy you like your job and all, but not all of us are having a good time at work right now and it's annoying to have you rub it in my face," he said. I was shocked. This same guy had listened to me endlessly complain about the lame menial tasks my other bosses had made me do when I was their assistants, including putting together all of one guy's IKEA furniture and picking up his living room rug and walking fifteen blocks through Soho with it slung over my shoulder because it wouldn't fit in a cab. I'd cried to him about how I'd been called a "useless twat" because I had bought the wrong kind of bagels for a morning meeting, and about how my next boss was just as mean and made me drive to IKEA with her one Saturday morning and then put together all of our office furniture. (Side note: I'm really good at putting together IKEA furniture.) So now I was finally excited about being on the right career track after years of floundering, and he was going to crush it? I was livid. I think I knew then and there that he wasn't the kind of guy you can envision your wedding and kids and grandkids with, all because he couldn't even fake being happy for me when something good came my way, just because he wasn't happy himself at the time.

So I completely understood when my friend said that her husband's enduring career support had made him marriage material. It's a very big deal for women. Supporting dreams, no matter how far-fetched, makes for a solid and potentially long-lasting partnership. That said, being realistic about dreams is also a pretty good quality for both parties to have. I once dated a guy who had so many ideas and schemes—open an animal sanctuary in Africa? Work as a bartender on a cruise ship?—that it was hard to keep his dreams straight, let alone support every single one of them. His dreams were stupid only because instead of doing anything to attain his goals, he smoked a lot of pot and drank Jack straight from the bottle.

Another friend of mine said she knew her husband was good marriage material because he was ridiculously honest with her. Yes, I know that being honest is one of those magazine article clichés, but there's something to it. Lying (either getting busted lying or finding out that your partner lied) is a really shitty sign that something isn't totally right. I'm not talking little white lies, which are most acceptable and encouraged as long as they are innocent. ("You are the most beautiful woman in all of Brooklyn" was one I used to get and really enjoy.) But I'm talking biggies—like "We're spending the bachelor party weekend whitewater rafting" when they're really going to Atlantic City. Anyway, my friend and her boyfriend had gone through a rough patch when dating, and he'd hooked up with another girl while out partying one night. The next day, in the midst of his horrible hangover and remorse, he cried his head off and told her about it, begging forgiveness.

"I walked out the fucking door," she told me. "I wasn't going to stick around after he'd just told me he bonked someone else, even if we were fighting and in the midst of deciding whether to stay together. Still, it was really rough to walk away from a year and a half of being together. I immediately missed him, but I was trying to find my anger instead of my sorrow so I could just get over him. The whole thing was awful."

Her boyfriend ended up checking into therapy and so did she for her own issues. A few weeks later they both began talking again, slowly at first. "It was really nice. He was so open and honest about all these feelings, and he'd been totally closed off before," she says. "Something about me leaving him combined with the therapy and the opening up for the first time in his life, and letting himself be vulnerable and crying in front of me—I don't know. It brought us even closer together. We ended up back together and moved in together about five months later and then got engaged five months after that. I guess I think he's marriage material because, one, he actually did tell me when he cheated and gave me a chance to decide what to do, which was kind of decent of him—not a lot of dudes do that. And two, since he started working on his issues, he's been this open, loving, kind guy who is super honest and thinks we should be able to talk about everything we're feeling with each other. That's also rare in a dude. He also just still seems so happy I gave him a second chance that we've been in this really gooey lovey-dovey phase for about two years now, and it doesn't seem to be slowing down. That's worth marrying for, that feeling of super mushy love. That's kind of what you aim for when you're prepping to walk down the aisle. It might not last, but to have that at least in the beginning is something to aim for."

Most other women I talked to said their husbands

were solid people and good friends and that they found them funny or cute and charming. They also had the same ideas about the future when it came to where they wanted to live, the kinds of things they wanted to attain (one friend of mine had a fiancé whose goal was to have a Porsche in three years and hers was to be pregnant with their first baby—things didn't end up that well), and most important, how they both felt about having children.

Dirty Girls tend to be smart women, thus acutely aware that the so-called perfect relationship doesn't actually exist. Men are men. There's not a single one of them out there who won't eventually annoy us, disgust us, disappoint us, and have some kind of penis problem from time to time. That guy you've conjured in your head, who always buys you pink tulips when they're in season and expensive purses just for the hell of it, either doesn't exist or will stop doing those things once he's fully conquered your heart and soul. So Dirty Girls don't go into a relationship expecting the guy to be perfect in every way, because they know that they themselves aren't perfect in every way. I'm certainly not perfect in every way, and I can be callous and insensitive and forgetful too. I even forgot the birthdays of my past two boyfriends and had to secretly check their driver's licenses when I knew the day was approaching. Would it have been a forgivable offense if I'd really forgotten their birthdays? Probably not—they'd be super pissed at me, and rightfully so.

In short, the perfect guy (or girl) isn't out there, and the best hope is that you can meet someone who is at least pretty close to perfect in your own eyes, whether that means he makes you breakfast in the mornings or lets you dress him up in stupid outfits for Halloween. Lowering expectations doesn't mean lowering standards or compromising your ideals—it means less disappointment in the long run and a better chance at actually grasping happiness. Perfect does not always mean it's for the best, anyway. And look, that way we don't have to feel so bad about our own shortcomings as women. I'm talking to you, Jaime, the girl who occasionally makes out with strangers at bars when her fiancé is out of town.

"Nothing is ever perfect," says one of my most trusted friends, who tells it like it is. "My husband is not one of those guys who rubs my feet and shoulders when I'm pregnant and fetches me drinks, and I know those guys exist because I see other women with them. Sometimes I wish he was, but then again, if he was I'd probably be like, 'Ugh, get off me and stop touching my damn feet all the time.' I just have to accept that this is the kind of guy I was attracted to enough to marry and deal with it. I make it work for me."

Which leads me to the next phase—how women *really* feel about babies.

Dirty Girls and Babies

It's not true that all women are born with a maternal instinct and every single one of us wants babies as soon as we can possibly have them. But it is true that we have a biological clock, and that little fucker really starts ticking somewhere around the late twenties or early thirties. For most people I know, they felt the first real baby pangs between twenty-eight and thirty-two. The older you get, the crueler Mother Nature is—she wants you to try and procreate, even if you haven't had a decent date in ages and much prefer sleeping in and eating late brunch on weekends than waking up at 5 a.m. to a pair of poopy pants. As a very lazy and not all that responsible Dirty Girl, I was shocked the day my biological clock suddenly decided to kick me in the ovaries when I was about thirty, and it was suddenly all I could do to not pat the head and kiss the cheek of every cutie patootie in a stroller that I saw. That shit came out of the blue, and it all took me aback.

"I want a baby!" I told my boyfriend that night, who looked at me weirdly and said, "We will someday, but just not now."

"Ugh no, I want one now," I whined. Then I caused a bad fight by saying that he never wanted kids and was wasting my time, and that if he truly felt that way and truly loved me he should set me free so I could find someone who shared my desire to procreate.

"You're being a crazy person," he told me, using his annoying go-to insult every time I did or said something that wasn't totally calm or rational.

"I'll show you crazy!" I said, actually being kind of crazy and throwing my cell phone at him from across the room and then running out to buy a pack of cigarettes and sit on the stoop with a bottle of wine and fume about how much I hated him because he didn't want to go ahead and have babies. Christ, the baby thing had suddenly really gotten under my skin.

Dirty Girls Who *Aren't* Ready for Babies

Just because I suddenly thought I *might* be getting ready to trade in good nights out with friends for *Goodnight Moon* didn't mean the majority of my friends felt the same way. When we talked about it, usually over cocktails, we generally concluded that babies were certainly something we wanted, but only in the safe and distant future. Even though we were starting to creep beyond the average mommy age, there was something not 100 percent appealing about giving up our independence and complete freedom. Even my friends who were married or in solid relationships felt this way. "It just seems… like a pointless pain in the *ass*," one of them said. "Totally," we mostly agreed.

While guys tend to think every chick over twenty-seven is on the mom path and might possibly be a sperm jacker (which is a really lame term they've given to girls they think are trolling bars when they're fertile so they'll get knocked up—as though every woman is dying to carry the spawn of a random guy she just met at a bar), the reality is that women are just as apprehensive when it comes to having children as men are, and just as often even more so than men. (Plus, every woman I spoke to agreed with this: the idea of being a single mom is absolutely terrifying.)

One of my friends once dated a guy who was really gung ho about getting hitched and having babies right away, and she couldn't bring herself around to his level of enthusiasm. "I couldn't handle it. All he did was talk about how he wanted babies and wanted to knock me up," she later told me. "We'd only been dating a few weeks and I kept explaining that I wasn't sure if I ever wanted children, but he wouldn't listen. Instead he'd say things like, 'But Frankie is a really cute name for either a boy or a girl, right?'" It didn't take her long before she just called things off with him. "Too much pressure!" she says.

Another of my friends let me know her feelings about babies a bit more succinctly. "Ick," she said. "I can't even imagine it. I'm still at a point where children annoy me. I just don't find them adorable, especially when they are in nice restaurants or crying on my flight. I hope that will change someday, but for now I am totally happy to not be a mom."

The Truth about Being Knocked Up

Not being able to drink and smoke and eat oysters seems like nothing compared to the joy of birth and babies and motherhood (blah, blah, blah), but to a lot of women, it seriously sucks to have these small joys taken away while they're up the duff, especially for women who are used to going to work and then going out for drinks with friends to catch up and blow off steam. You won't hear many people admitting to this, as pregnant women are supposed to be happy and nesting. But it's the truth.

Suddenly being told that you need to find some other, healthier outlet in which to chill out from a long day can be pretty hard. Sure, there's the gym, but when you're pregnant, and especially at the beginning, you don't really want to go exercise. There are dinners out, but in the beginning you'll just be bummed you can't enjoy a nice glass of wine alongside everyone else, food grosses you out anyway, and socializing when you'd rather be in the bath is lame. There's a serious mourning period for losing this part of your life—women need to learn to let go of years and years of a regular behavioral pattern, even if it's only for nine months or for however long it is until they stop breast-feeding.

That alone is enough to scare some Dirty Girls away from having a baby for a while.

Perfect Careers

Like the perfect man, there is no such thing as the perfect job. There are fantastic jobs and wonderful ways to make money, and I'm sure there are some people who are so happy with what they do that they feel like they don't even have jobs. I do not personally know these people, but I assume they are probably skydiving instructors and founders of exotic travel companies for rich adventurers. Still, I'm sure the skydiving instructor has had bitches of days where his clients were awful, he just didn't want to get out of bed, or the chute didn't open. And I bet the exotic travel company lady has also had days where she was like, "Ugh, I don't want to get on a first-class seat on a plane and go hiking up Mount Kilimanjaro this week. I want to stay home with a bowl of cereal in bed and watch *Friends* reruns!" OK, maybe not, but there's always hope out there for the rest of us who are in jobs that aren't always exactly ideal.

Even that dream job I had, the one where my boyfriend pooh-poohed my happiness? I had plenty of crap to gripe about, from having to make photocopies for freelance writers to ordering lunch for some of the senior editors. Oh, and did I mention I was twenty-seven and my annual salary was less in thousands than my age? As with everything else, you have to take your career prospects with a grain of salt. For every position you covet, there is something that will be wrong with it. I used to be so envious of a girl I knew who spent most of her time doing these awesome travel stories for a cool magazine. I imagined she just had the most perfect life in every way. She was pretty, she was cool, and she made good money doing assignments all over the world. I wanted her life! Then I actually had an assignment where I was sent somewhere exotic, and as exciting as it was, by the second day I was really lonely and decided that traveling alone wasn't really my thing. I'd always had traveling companions before, and I was bored and found myself longing to get back to dirty ol' Brooklyn and my friends. When I did return, I felt a little bit better about my own semistalled career—the grass is always greener, and I suddenly had one fewer person's career to envy. Still, if only they paid me just a *little* bit more at my current job… That's another thing that Dirty

Girls—just like men—always have an issue with: money. We often feel like there's never enough, and there's never an easy way for us to make *more*— going on Craigslist and selling your dirty panties to perverted old men notwithstanding.

When I was younger, a colleague of mine and I used to sit around and talk about how all we needed in life was to make a salary of $80,000 a year, and then we'd know we'd made it and life could be complete. We were, at the time, making $27,000 a year, and the idea that we could one day bring home that much bacon was amazing. Time went on, and though I still never managed to attain that as a base salary, she did and more. She ended up making six figures, and I wondered whether she thought she had made it and life was complete. She could shop for clothes when she wanted, she had a huge pile of savings stashed away, and she had her own apartment. Over drinks, I asked whether she thought everything was perfect now that she had made such good money.

"Eh," she said. "You can always have more. I don't know what I was thinking when I said all I needed was $80,000 a year to be happy. It really doesn't seem to be that much money now."

Jesus. As long as I kept equating money with life success, I would never be happy!

And so I learned not to think that if only I had a little bit more, then things would be a little bit better. Which was smart, considering I was working in one of the fastest dying fields out there: magazine writing.

Accepting or Being Very Happy with the Way Things Are

It's rare to come across a Dirty Girl who admits that she is perfectly *elated* with the way her life has worked out, but it's certainly not rare to come across women who are perfectly *happy*. The majority of us often have moments when we wonder what it would be like on the other side, whether that's married, or single, or working as a waitress in Europe and sleeping with lots of hot men, or being a filthy-rich executive, or being a stay-at-home mom…The possibilities of life paths we could have taken are truly endless. And for tons of women I know, the possibilities still are. I have a sister who decided two years ago that fuck it, she was sick of being an executive in New York and wanted to live in L.A. and be by the beach for a while, so she did just that. Another friend of mine decided, fuck it, she was sick of pretending she was into guys and wanted to be herself, which is a foxy lesbian who allows herself to be as dramatic as she damn well pleases without having to hear "You're crazy" from another man again. But I asked all my friends if they considered themselves happy, and every single one of them replied, "Yes. Well, most of the time, anyway."

That means that despite everything we could be doing differently, most of us feel like we're doing what's right for us. Waking up day after day with the same guy who is starting to annoy us? The same commute to the same stupid job where we have to kiss ass to our same stupid boss? It's actually not all that bad. "If I was truly unhappy, I'd do something about it," one woman told me. "There's nothing stopping me from packing up and moving to Guatemala to teach English, which I threaten to do every single winter," she says. "But at the end of the day, I have my friends here and I really do have a lot of fun things happening in my life, even though I can spend hours complaining about shit. I actually pretty much love everything about my life."

HAVE YOUR MAN READ THIS, PLEASE:
HAPPILY EVER AFTER

Guys, you might think that we're not all that happy because we like to complain about shit. But it's simply not true. It's just that griping and voicing our opinions about who is annoying and what we hate is, for whatever reason, super *fun*. Like a juicy piece of gossip, bitching is exciting and a way to get our frustration out without actually having to do anything physical like go to the gym.

Of course there are women who seem to constantly whine about this and that. But for the average Dirty Girl, bitching doesn't make us bitches, nor does it mean we're necessarily unhappy about anything. If we were, we would simply find the energy and strength to change things. No, we're a pretty content group of humans. Dirty Girls may be secretly filthy, we may be somewhat lazy, and we may sometimes lie and drink too much, but one thing we're not is miserable. Because at the end of the day, it's actually pretty great being a girl.

And we hope you never want us to change

a single thing about our great, and completely nasty, selves.

About the Author

*G*illian Telling is a sex columnist for *Maxim*, where she tells men how women think. She has written for *Rolling Stone* and *Details*, and she regularly writes for thefrisky.com.